Organizing for Marketing Advantage

SALES AND MARKETING STRUCTURES FOR THE EUROPE OF THE 1990S

Prepared and published by **Business International Ltd**
A member of The Economist Group
40 Duke Street, London W1A 1DW
United Kingdom

ISBN 0 85058 366 7

Preface

With more than 440 million people, the emerging "Greater" Europe is potentially the dominant trading bloc in the world, but it is divided into many different markets. While multinational managements have already begun to rationalize their research and development and production facilities across Europe as a whole, there is still much experimentation and doubt about the most effective way of organizing the marketing and sales operations.

In this report, the experiences of more than 40 multinational companies are described in detail, and an analysis made of the problems and pressures they face in their European operations, the underlying purposes their organizations are designed to fulfill, and the numerous structures that have evolved to achieve their ends. Of course, every company's style is different, as well as its markets and ambitions, and slavish copying of an organizational structure would be dangerous. But as the responses from the companies that cooperated in this study amply indicate, many organizational problems are common to many companies, and the number of possible solutions to them is limited.

But these "solutions" are appropriate only as long as the underlying conditions and assumptions remain unchanged, and there is every sign that the rate of change will quicken as the European markets evolve, the product life cycle shortens, and the investment demanded and financial pressures on managements to perform increase. If this report helps managements to shorten the odds in their favor, it will have achieved its purpose.

The author and Business International would like to thank all the companies and consultants who contributed to the study, in particular Unilever plc, Colgate-Palmolive Europe, Heinz, IBM, and the Ashridge Strategic Management Centre, London.

The report was researched and written by Tom Lester, consultant and specialist writer on business affairs.

Table of Contents

Part II: Europe and the Marketing Matrix

Chapter 4: The Objectives of European Organization

Chapter 5: The Future of the Country Manager

Chapter 6: Coordinators and the Product Manager

Chapter 7: The Matrix and Beyond

Part III: Scale and Diversity

Chapter 8: Targeting Sales and Prices

Chapter 9: Keeping Control: the Impact of Information Technology

Chapter 10: The Human Factor

Part IV: Conclusions

Chapter 11: Conclusions

Executive Summary

The global setting

Multinational companies operating in Europe are engaged in rethinking and sometimes fundamentally changing their marketing and sales structures. Of the more than 40 multinational companies covered in this report, over half have significantly altered their European marketing operations in the past two years. Their aim is to improve customer response while at the same time planning on a continental scale. Most of the changes have been toward more devolution, and striking the right balance between central and local control—which many view as the key issue.

With some 440 million people, the emerging "Greater" Europe is potentially the dominant consumption bloc in the world, but it is divided into numerous individual markets. Competitive advantage and the EC's Internal Market Program are two stimuli to reorganize. Others are:

- the collapse of communism and moves toward free-market economies in Eastern and Central Europe, adding a further group of potential markets which may overload the present structure;

- hostile takeover threats, which have prompted cuts in noncore activities and led to concentration on international brands and selective acquisitions;

- the realization by a number of companies that hands-on management of a diverse European empire simply does not work;

- the diversity of conditions in European markets, producing differential growth rates;

- changes in the way products have to be marketed, often demanding greater local autonomy but more coordination;

- the growing consciousness of purchasing power among international buying groups and multinational customers, stimulating demands for Europewide, even global, prices and standards of service.

The role of the center has changed substantially in response to these pressures. The unpredictability of world events, rapid technological change and portfolio management are leading to slimmer central functions. At the European level, many companies have also decided to reduce the size of the regional office. Nevertheless, all of the non-European multinationals featured in the report regard a small European office as an essential extension of the head office. In the process of change, the role of the center has become more sharply defined. As far as marketing and sales operations in Europe are concerned, five key functions stand out: focusing resources and organization on key products and markets; securing a flow of new products and application technologies to the field operations; selecting managers suited to a complex European structure; selecting and propagating best practice; and monitoring performance.

An effective corporate structure must reflect the group's European objectives. Apart from overall profitability, issues critical in its design are the limited ability or experience of the local management; the need to maximize returns from R&D and product ideas; the economies of scale in manufacturing and distribution; the cumulative strength of international branding; utilization of the available management talent and ideas; serving international customers; cutting advertising costs; and growing competition across European markets.

Europe and the marketing matrix

Some or all of these issues are in managers' minds when deciding how to adapt the classical organizational forms—functional, product and geographical divisions, or some combination. Specific motives include:

- to meet changing market needs—GKN, Levi Strauss;

- to encourage future growth—Compaq;

- to boost profit—Renault, SKF;

- to assert a European perspective—Colgate-Palmolive, Unilever and United Distillers;

- to improve speed and maneuverability—3M, Reckitt & Colman;

- to minimize bureaucracy—Heinz, Jacobs Suchard and Eurotherm.

Moves to coordinate European marketing have been seen as a threat to the country manager. Often vital to profitable growth, country managers are typically entrepreneurs with considerable power based on profit contribution. But they are limited to their own countries, and can be a barrier to pan-European operations and compete with each other. Moves to rationalize manufacturing and distribution across Europe may erode much of their responsibility; they may also limit sensitivity to local market trends and needs. Although most companies are aiming to coordinate their marketing across Europe, only one company in this report has taken profit responsibility away from its country managers. In fact, companies are currently seeking to enhance the use of country operations through the lead country system, whereby one subsidiary Europewide is given responsibility for a specific product, application or tactic. The danger of the lead country system lies in the confusion over responsibilities, which has led some consumer goods companies to prefer other routes.

Most companies see a growing need to coordinate their sales and marketing between products and across Europe to check costs and competitors. It can be done without additional staff or structures, but many companies prefer formal methods:

- **Coordinators:** They pull together subsidiaries' marketing, but they generally do not have enough power to force through major changes.

- **Product managers:** In business marketing, large international product divisions can be insensitive to shifts in the marketplace. Also, the responsibility for markets outside the product division is often unclear, allied products from different divisions may compete with each other, and country market shares may be sacrificed to divisional profitability. In consumer goods, product managers are becoming more common, but powers and relationships with country managers are delicate.

- **Advertising** offers a useful clue as to the real balance between the center and its outposts. Agencies have to adapt their output and their own structures to meet clients' needs. They have to provide a channel for international marketing spending, guard the central "brand values" and provide ideas suitable for Europewide application. Some clients prefer one or two international agencies to simplify and strengthen European coordination. Others put creative quality first, and hire the best available agency for the local market. Most surveyed companies used a combination of the two policies.

- **The matrix:** As responsibilities between product and country managers approach equilibrium, a matrix is formed as a means of rationalizing natural product/geographical conflicts. At least one third of the companies in the report rely on some kind of matrix, but the bureaucracy has deterred most from a balanced matrix in which both axes are given profit responsibility.

- **The matrix plus:** 3M has set up European management action teams (Emats) for 40 product groups. Chaired by a subsidiary product manager, the Emat acts as a product management forum, while leaving the country manager's profit responsibility intact. At Lever Europe, European brand groups report to the detergents chief executive and consist of executives based in country subsidiaries. They formulate the marketing mix and "sell" it to the national brand managers, who report for profit performance through their country managers to the chief executive.

Japanese companies in the survey use a loose, informal organization, but with a lot of committees and a strong culture. Other variants on the geographic/product theme include:

- **Strategic links:** Strategy and crises demand the best brainpower and experience. Country managers can supply both if they are part of the top European board or committee.

- **Task forces:** Special-purpose committees, teams, groups or task forces appear to be growing in number and importance. They save staff but can waste time and be difficult to control.

- **The network potential:** Management networks (not to be confused with information technology networks) are gaining ground as an idea, but practical experience of them is limited and they depend on a high level of IT sophistication.

Scale and diversity

Although selling and pricing are likely to remain essentially local, they have to conform to customers' evolving demands. Coordination across frontiers is becoming necessary for international customers, and corporate expertise must be mobilized to solve customers' problems. Prices must be set to meet local conditions as well as the wider European needs.

Few companies are satisfied with their sales structures. There are difficulties connecting the sales operations into the marketing matrix. Eurosales teams to interface with central buying units are still rare and sales volumes small. Multinational customers that buy locally may expect international standards of service while offering sales opportunities in other countries. To exploit this, several companies use the lead country system; a few use international account managers. Localized sales structures can inhibit access to the increasingly open public procurement markets in the EC.

A modern European corporate structure demands an equally modern information network. Several companies in this survey are upgrading their systems or planning major investment. The style of control determines the information demanded—and Japanese companies differ markedly from US and UK companies in this respect. Most current information systems have grown out of the accounts department, with varying purposes and standards. An up-to-date system allows better control, and scope to push decision making much nearer to the customer. But even the most modern IT networks cannot ensure that data mean what they purport to mean. For that, the center has to rely on the integrity of executives, and frequent field visits.

Flexible management structures and networks cannot function without adequate data availability, and lateral as well as vertical flow. This is therefore a priority. Radical improvements in the data network are partly dependent on parallel improvements in distribution and administration. Within the EC, the removal of barriers will allow cuts in the number of warehouses and delivery times. Improved communications will allow administration centers to be rationalized also, and located wherever convenient.

Operating effectively in a modern European organization requires human skills, flexibility and vision which the companies in the survey have found to be scarce. Radical change in responsibilities and patterns of working demand care, and sometimes changes in personnel.

- **Job experience:** Transferring executives from one country to another is still rare, and getting more, not less, difficult. More common is to give executives two roles, a national and a European one.

- **Remuneration:** Carefully constructed bonus systems are frequently used to keep managers' eyes focused on European as well as national performance. The most sophisticated reward global, European, national and personal performance in a precise formula.

- **Travel:** For some key executives, European coordination imposes a very heavy travel burden. Dual roles will increase the need for travel, and overall, the time and cost is likely to grow, mitigated only by improved IT systems such as electronic mail and teleconferencing.

Part I
The Global Setting

Chapter 1

Introduction

> "Every time we talk about strategy, we end up talking about organization."
>
> Trevor Holdsworth, former chairman, GKN

Very few companies are in the fortunate position of being able to plan their organizations on a blank piece of paper. The great majority already have assets on the ground, employees, customers, cultures and technologies that combine to provide something near the desired commercial result. For these companies, the first question that has to be asked is therefore not what organization should it adopt, but how should it change to face the challenges of the 1990s?

In a subject as fluid as corporate organization, there can be no finite answers. What suits the needs, the people and the aspirations of one company will not suit those of another; what is written down in neat organization charts may or may not correspond to practical, day-to-day reality; what suits a company in an aggressive expansionary phase may not work when conditions alter. For all that, there are basic, underlying problems with which all multinational corporations (MNCs) have to contend, and these problems are perhaps more acute in marketing and sales operations in Europe than anywhere else. Furthermore, the solutions they have adopted can be seen as variations on relatively few themes. This report examines the issues involved in organizing sales and marketing structures based on the experience of senior executives in more than 40 major MNCs*, and the solutions they currently adopt.

It is significant that of the companies covered, 57% are operating through organizations that are either new or have been significantly modified in the past two years; nearly a third have made important changes since research for this report began. Of the newly modified organizations, the intention in half of the companies has been to decentralize power, insofar as this has any meaning in the modern MNC. In contrast, centralizing power accounted for less than a quarter; the rest opted for some kind of coordinating matrix.

---

* Companies include Aegis, Agip, Alitalia, Amex, ASSI, Audi, Bang & Olufsen, Black & Decker, BOC, BP, Canon, Ciba-Geigy, Colgate-Palmolive, Compaq, Digital Equipment, Du Pont, Electrolux, Eurotherm, GKN, Glaxo, Heinz, Hoechst, Honeywell, IBM, ICI Europa, Jacobs Suchard, Kodak, Lego, Lever Europe, Levi Strauss, 3M, Moulinex, NCR, Nestlé, L'Oréal, Osram, Procter & Gamble, Rank Xerox, Renault, Roche, Scott Paper, SKF, TI Group, Union Carbide and United Distillers.

European Trading Blocs

Organizing for Marketing Advantage
Business International

THE GREATER EUROPEAN MARKET

		Population (million)	GDP ($ billion, 1989)
EC:	Belgium	9.9	151
	Denmark	5.1	104
	France	56.2	948
	Greece	10.1	54
	Ireland	3.7	33
	Italy	57.3	866
	Luxembourg	0.4	7
	Netherlands	14.8	223
	Portugal	10.3	45
	Spain	39.3	377
	UK	56.9	827
	West Germany	60.5	1,196
Efta:	Austria	7.5	126
	Finland	5.0	116
	Iceland	0.3	5
	Norway	4.2	93
	Sweden	8.3	190
	Switzerland	6.5	175
Eastern Europe	Czechoslovakia	15.7	154*
	East Germany	16.7	207*
	Hungary	10.6	92*
	Poland	38.4	276*

*1988.
Sources: UN, OECD, IMF, CIA, *The Economist.*

The European dimension

Europe is a microcosm of global business, and many of the corporate issues that companies raise when describing their European structures are not confined to Europe. With 18 states making up the proposed European Community/European Free Trade Association European Economic Space, along with some of the new market economies of the former Eastern bloc, companies are faced with a unique organizational problem. There are some 440 million consumers divided into any number of separate markets. Yet Europe is potentially the dominant consumption bloc in the world, and the companies that win in Europe are likely to reign supreme in world markets. The big puzzle is finding the right organization to profit from such a large but fragmented area, and knowing when to harmonize and when to exploit the differences.

The EC's Internal Market Program, which is scheduled to be completed on the last day of 1992, is probably the *least* important of the reasons for the current surge of restructuring activity among MNCs. Crucial differences will persist for several decades. A more simple stimulus is the growing realization that an effective marketing structure is not just a vital

THE SNARE OF CLASSIFICATION

The attempt to classify companies by type of organization is as perilous as classifying people—each one is unique, and for practical purposes, superficial resemblances are as likely to mislead as to guide. In the following lists, companies judged to be instructive examples of a particular characteristic are grouped together, but the lists are not intended to be in any way definitive.

Strong country managers

(i.e. relatively little operational interference from the center)

Canon	Nestlé
Compaq	Rank Xerox
Eurotherm	Roche
GKN Chep	TI John Crane
L'Oréal	IBM

Strong central authority

Agip	Gillette
Lego	Thorn Lighting
Union Carbide	

Recently decentralized

Alitalia	Ciba-Geigy
Hoechst	IBM
Rank Xerox	SKF

Balanced matrix

(i.e. profit responsibility divided between geographical and product axes)

Electrolux	Honeywell
Kodak	NCR
Procter & Gamble	

Loose matrix

(i.e. evolving into product/country matrix)

Colgate-Palmolive	Jacobs Suchard (sale negotiated)
Moulinex	

Integrated Eurostructure

(i.e. strong country managers, undivided profit responsibility, small central staff but close liaison)

Black & Decker	Heinz
Reckitt & Colman	Scott

prerequisite of corporate health; it can provide the key to powerful competitive advantage. And lessons learned in Europe are being applied elsewhere.

Why coordinate?

Despite the growing perception of Europe as a single economic entity, it is important to avoid the assumption that a closely coordinated European operation is necessarily the right objective. The results will not always justify the costs, however they are measured. The minimum of interference and control over executives who are able and trustworthy is often a more effective policy. For most of the companies in this survey, however, their operations are too widespread and complex to allow such a luxury. Specifically, they are aiming to:

- increase sensitivity to the market;

- realize the benefits of pan-European scale, in terms of production, distribution, advertising, administration etc;

- mobilize more effectively the ideas and skills of their executives, wherever they are based;

- turn the promise of modern information technology (IT) into a competitive advantage.

Few companies in the survey claimed to be anywhere near to enjoying the real benefits of IT, and many were daunted by the size of the task ahead of them. IT implies not just substantial investments in hardware and software, but also corresponding changes in attitudes and working practices. Indeed, the introduction of IT strategies is facilitating changes in corporate organization toward ad hoc groupings and networks, and away from departments and hierarchies. Many themes have yet to be fully explored, let alone exploited. For several companies, however, there is no doubt that this is where the future lies, even though at this stage it may be an act of faith (see Chapter 9).

The battle front

A far-flung MNC, with sales and marketing companies in a number of countries, suffers from the same problem of large organizations throughout history. The center may decree, instruct or advise, but it can be certain that at least some of the outposts will not obey. The reasons may be bad ones—pride, pigheadness or a simple mistake—but they may also be good ones. The center cannot know all the circumstances faced by its field commanders day-to-day, and economic, competitive or other pressures may suddenly change in one or two territories. Policies painfully reached on the best advice may simply be inappropriate by the time they are applied at the battle front.

That was one reason that prompted **Rank Xerox**, the worldwide arm of the US Xerox Corp, to abandon attempts to devise marketing strategies for use by its operating companies from its regional headquarters in the UK. In theory, executives would provide a "center of competence," drawing on the best practice worldwide, on which the rest of the organization could draw in its turn. In practice, Japanese competitors, without such lofty ambitions, never allowed it that luxury.

Centralize or decentralize?

"One of the major topics in IBM," says a senior executive explaining the company's moves to decentralize, "is the balance between central power and local authority. It was always important, but now the industry is restructuring and so are customers." Achieving this balance is particularly pressing for the sales and marketing functions, where managements face the crucial problem of ensuring close and flexible attention to customers' needs at the same time as planning their operations on a global scale. Other corporate functions such as research and development, manufacturing, and finance have organizational problems of their own, but do not have to strive for the same delicate central/local balance.

To "think global and act local," as many companies claim to do, begs the question of what is the one and what the other, and whether the organization will allow the process to be carried through effectively without risking corporate schizophrenia. The amount of reorganization activity being undertaken by the companies in this survey suggests that in many cases the ideal is a long way from attainment.

Furthermore, the clear trend toward more flexible, task-oriented structures removes the last vestiges of meaning from the conventional distinction between centralized and decentralized structures. None of the companies in this study can be said to fit into either category—all of them have elements of both, even within the same function. In one company, the pack design might be determined by the center but the advertising for it left entirely to the local subsidiary. In another, strategy might be a central concern but its actual formulation left to the country managers in committee.

Of course, there are the essentially centralized Coca-Colas and McDonald's on the one side, and the faceless, highly decentralized conglomerates like Hanson of the UK or the Suez-controlled Société Générale de Belgique on the other. The organizational issue becomes a matter for serious debate for the great majority of companies lying between those two extremes. It is these companies that form the subject of this study. They have a variety of products or services in any given market segment, and marketing and sales operations in a number of countries; their operations will benefit from some degree of coordinated management.

The evidence from this study suggests that they are becoming more centralized and more decentralized at one and the same time.

- **Increasing centralization:** The central management team, conscious that it may be called upon to make radical changes in the composition and direction of the company at short notice, has designed the basic, central structure to facilitate acquisition, divestment etc.

- **Increasing decentralization:** Companies are also devolving more power to operational managers, to allow them to respond more effectively to market demands.

The losers in the whole process are the middle echelons, which planned and forecast, and coordinated and analyzed, but which top managers have decided that they now can do without.

The matrix in the mind

Academic management theorists have drawn a distinction between multinationals and "transnationals"—a term coined by two specialists, Christopher Bartlett and Sumantra Ghoshal. They conclude their study *Managing Across Borders* with the statement: "In the future, a company's ability to develop a transnational organizational capability will be the key factor that separates the winners from the mere survivors in the international competitive environment."

What they mean by a transnational organization is one where the basic matrix structure found in practically all multinational companies is softened and simplified by common sense and the unifying force of corporate purpose. Social contact and "a matrix in the minds of managers" replace many of the more bureaucratic and unwieldy structures, and the process of reaching decisions is varied according to their implications, rather than following a formal set of rules.

Some might see this description as closely fitting the way certain major European and Japanese companies such as Nestlé, Electrolux, ICI or Canon have conducted their affairs all along: "Our employee always has a roundtable in his mind; he is always free to stand up and say what he wants. This is typically Japanese: everybody takes part in the decision making," says the manager of a Japanese consumer electronics company. Bartlett, a professor of business administration at Harvard, seems to be arguing against the generalizations and authoritarian style of some US corporations rather than the more pragmatic, consensus management style favored by some European and Japanese companies.

The latter are perhaps better accustomed to dealing with the differentiation and complexities of the European markets, so unlike the large and relatively homogeneous US domestic market which still influences the organization of many US multinationals. Both styles have their virtues; but corporate managements need to be aware of the cultural differences, and judge accordingly the cultural background of management consultants and academics, as well as the advice they provide.

The transnational hypothesis chimes with the analysis provided by Peters and Waterman in the 1982 book *In Search of Excellence*. This emphasized autonomy and entrepreneurship in small business units controlled by a lean head office with few administrative layers. But the Peters and Waterman advocacy of "loose-tight" management control—loose on, say, sales tactics, while tight on strategy or cash management—is no more than the long-standing practice of many of the companies in this study. It is also in tune with the increase in competitiveness in many markets, and the rising imperative of winning the battle customer by customer, market segment by market segment.

Justifying the trauma

This report shows that for even the most sophisticated companies, a radical reorganization is not only a traumatic experience but, in terms of the benefits, it is often an act of faith. Few companies are as confident as **SKF**, the Swedish world leader in roller bearings, which attributed much of its 63% increase in 1989 group profits to its new organizational structure, now three years old. **3M** still wonders whether it would have been pushed out of the office copier business by the Japanese had its present organizational structure been in place in the 1970s. But for most, the cost-benefit equation remains insoluble, and the only certainty is the danger of doing nothing.

The German computer company **Nixdorf**, for example, was once the darling of the German stock market, but was taken over by Siemens in early 1990 after making 1989 losses of over Dm1 billion ($642 million). Observers believe that one of the main reasons for Nixdorf's decline was its maintenance of its old, regionally based organization. Although it eventually changed to an organization focusing on market segments (such as banking, retail etc.) like many other computer firms, the change came too late. Similarly, the UK management services group **Saatchi & Saatchi**, for a time the largest advertising agency in the world, failed to develop its international structure in line with its ambitions and its rapid growth, leading to inadequate cost control and 1989 losses of £56 million ($100 million).

The importance of history

For many companies, the origins of their present organization date back a very long way. However, company organization should never be seen as a fixture, but as a constantly evolving living organism. At least two of the US companies that participated in this study, **Eastman Kodak** and **NCR**, were already established in Europe in 1900. For the first two thirds of this century, they were controlled closely by their US headquarters working through national manufacturing and sales subsidiaries. The structure made good sense, and enabled them to dominate the European photographic and cash register markets respectively.

But technologies, markets and competition have all altered radically since then, and both giants have had to adapt their organizations to suit. NCR's transmutation from a company based on electromechanical technology to electronics was hastened, if not caused, by the laxity of its organization. Its Japanese subsidiary grew impatient with the US headquarters' failure to develop an electronic till, and decided to produce its own. Eventually, Tokyo general manager Bill Anderson was summoned back to HQ and given the job of converting the whole company to electronics—and saving it from extinction. This illustrates effectively that a centralized organization depends vitally on the center knowing what it is doing; if it doesn't, disorganization may be a positive advantage.

Less is more

In fact, fuzzier, informal organizations where executives readily cross boundaries (if the interests of the business dictate it) can be more effective than rigid, clear-cut ones, particularly in a region like Europe. Our survey has produced examples of companies favoring both formal and informal structures—the latter seemingly a Japanese characteristic, where heavy reliance is placed on the corporate culture and individuals' long experience of working together. Whichever type is preferred, it is safe to conclude that less organization rather than more is the desired goal. Simplicity is its own virtue.

Chapter 2

Pressures for Organizational Change

Management, like politics, is the art of the possible. Many wonderful organizations have been devised, only to be short-circuited at the first crisis when simple, straightforward relationships, short lines of communication and concentration on essentials are required. The threat of economic recession is often enough to kill off coordinating committees and dotted-line relationships with abrupt finality. If sales targets are in doubt, the line management-sales force axis tends to have priority whatever the regulations may say. If radical change becomes imperative, the central planners hold sway.

The combined experience of the companies taking part in this report points to two separate sources of pressure that are having a profound bearing on European marketing and sales structures. There are the broad macro forces external to the company that shape the context for doing business. These can include moves such as the EC's 1992 program or the wave of liberalization in Central and Eastern Europe. In addition, there are the issues specific to micro sectors or businesses, and within each company, particular forces will be at work, such as differential progress between marketing regions, that shape the structure and organization.

In practice, of course, the macro and micro forces interact with the company's corporate strategy. The resulting structure has to be strong and resilient enough to support continuous profitable growth. A significant change in any one of many macro and micro factors could require at the very least that the corporate structure be reexamined, and at the most that radical change be implemented.

External Macro Pressures

The Internal Market Program*

The combined impact of the EC's decision to remove the remaining nontariff barriers to free trade and competition within the Community may be summarized as follows:

☐ The gradual harmonization of standards will increase the quantity and range of products sold across national boundaries. Companies are therefore rationalizing their production between, typically, two or three plants covering the whole region in order to take advantage of the new economies of scale possible. Company subsidiaries that once controlled their own manufacturing now have to draw their products from a

---

* This subject has been covered in detail in Business International's research report *The 1993 Company: Corporate Strategies for Europe's Single Market*.

central source. This means a new degree of coordination with fellow subsidiaries. Black & Decker is a prime example.

□ The physical distribution of goods is being concentrated on a few central warehouses, with major implications for internal systems (see Chapter 9).

□ Companies are putting resources behind products and brands that have international status or potential. As a result, marketing structures need to be redesigned to accommodate both international and local brands (see Chapter 5).

In addition, issues such as differential pricing place new demands on marketing structures, as the following example illustrates:

Ecosystem is a French auto dealer that specializes in buying vehicles for domestic customers in the cheapest European market. At the moment, widening discrepancies exist between France, Belgium, Denmark, Germany etc., which manufacturers explain away by the need to conform to different national technical standards. Peugeot is typical in trying to keep its markets segregated, and in May 1989 instructed its agents in Belgium and Luxembourg not to supply Ecosystem. The European Commission, however, has insisted that Peugeot supply Ecosystem with up to 1,200 autos a year (Ecosystem's purchase volume before the ban) pending a detailed investigation. Pressure on the manufacturers is expected to increase.

Opportunities in Central and Eastern Europe

Dominating many company executives' thoughts since the peoples' revolutions of 1989 is Central and Eastern Europe, and the rapidly changing prospects the region now offers. It is too early, and events are moving too fast, for companies to have made significant changes to their structures to allow them to develop the new opportunities opening up. However, the extension of the definition of "the European market" eastward needs to be kept in mind when contemplating structural changes in the West. The incorporation of East Germany with West, alongside the growing links with Poland, Czechoslovakia, Hungary, Romania, Bulgaria, Yugoslavia and, of course, the Soviet Union will eventually shift the center of economic gravity eastward. As a result, Brussels may lose some of its popularity to Vienna or Berlin as a base for a European regional headquarters.

For political reasons, joint ventures are likely to figure prominently, since perceived national interests exercise just as powerful a tug as in the West. However, several companies, the Swedish giant **Electrolux** among them, do not conceal their dislike of joint ventures because of the confusion in objectives and control that is a common feature.

As for organic expansion in Eastern Europe, German groups like Siemens or Volkswagen could cease to consider East Germany as a foreign territory the moment the Berlin Wall came down, and plan for it as part of their domestic market. But whatever the pace of political unification, East Germany may for most companies justify separate organizational structures for some years to come, owing to its economic and political heritage.

Most non-German multinationals are, like **NCR**, reacting cautiously to developments. For the time being, NCR is simply extending its structure eastward by setting up branch offices

THE MERGER MAELSTROM

Fear of takeover, and the generally tougher investment climate in most financial centers have prompted some MNCs, particularly those originating in the US, to reorganize their European operations as part of a major exercise to improve financial performance. Deciding what are the core businesses is now the customary first stage in the remedial action; second comes divestment of what are deemed to be peripheral activities; last is reorganizing the core to make it leaner and more effective—or simply better able to support the debt burden that may have been incurred.

■ **Gillette**, a victim of "greenmail" in the mid–1980s and still vulnerable to market adventurers, was forced in defending itself to triple its corporate debt to reach a peak debt/equity ratio of nearly 200%. In an attempt to recover its poise, it has divested itself of a long string of businesses, the latest announced in January 1990, aimed at cutting costs in the remaining European shaving and male toiletries businesses by heavily centralizing its marketing in a North Atlantic Shaving & Personal Care Group. The effectiveness of this latter move will be measured in part by the success of its 19-nation launch this year of the new wet-shaving system, Sensor.

■ **Kodak** has not suffered so severely from corporate raiders, but much of the impetus behind its reorganization in the 1980s came from the imperative need to improve its financial performance. The changes will be detailed later (see Chapter 6), but Wall Street is evidently still not satisfied with the financial results.

Where acquisition rather than divestment is the priority, a tighter organization may again be required, but for a different reason. Successful acquisitions in today's competitive conditions require:

• a clear strategic sense based on a careful analysis of the group's strengths and weaknesses;

• a united management team attuned to decisive action;

• painstaking field intelligence to locate possible targets and assess their strengths and weaknesses, and therefore the potential "fit"; and

• mobilization of cash and other financial resources to enable the group to mount the bid.

■ **Unilever**, for all its financial success, boasted none of these in the 1960s. It had relied largely on the organic growth of its highly autonomous and widely spread operating subsidiaries. Financial management was similarly relaxed, and one or two small but significant takeover bids in the UK failed. But by the late 1970s, it had set up a US regional headquarters, and bought critical mass in the US marketplace with the purchase of National Starch, paying what was then the highest price ever for a US company by a foreigner. Ten years later, with a much tighter central management team, it mounted a rapid and ultimately successful bid for the Chesebrough-Pond's personal products group, having earlier been beaten to the draw for Richardson-Vicks by its arch rival, Procter & Gamble.

Such acquisitions raise vital questions about how they should be attached to the existing structure. Much depends on the company's overall strategy and management style, as well as the more obvious considerations of line of business, size and location of the ⇨

acquired assets etc. In the Chesebrough-Pond's case, Unilever determined to amalgamate the purchased operations with its existing Elida Gibbs personal care business, but whether Chesebrough-Ponds was merged into Gibbs or vice versa depended on which unit was the larger in each European country.

■ By contrast, when the US food group **Heinz** bought the Weight Watchers (WW) operation in 1978, there was considerable internal debate as to how such a distinct business should be fitted in to Heinz's worldwide organization. At the time of the takeover, WW's slimming foods and Heinz's own products were sold through largely similar outlets. As a result, if the two were merged, Heinz's marketing skills could be expected to expand WW's sales. However, Heinz decided to separate the "classroom group" (essentially about organizing educational weight loss programs in the community) from the high-street operations. Heinz's senior vice president, Europe, Paul Corddry, explains that grocery products like ketchup, baked beans, baby foods and the WW range require a hard sell to make an impact in the supermarkets. A small coordinating group was appointed from both sides at the operating level. WW now provides an operating income of over $100 million annually.

in Poland, Czechoslovakia, Hungary etc. via its West German subsidiary. Many managements, however, may find that the European region will still need to be subdivided because of size, either geographically (northern and southern states, for example) or economically (by gross national product per head).

Soaps and detergents group **Colgate-Palmolive** has decided to take the plunge with a separate organization for the whole of Central and Eastern Europe (except for East Germany, which will be handled by the West German subsidiary). As Brussels-based Brian Bergin, president of Colgate-Palmolive Europe, explains: "A whole different set of circumstances applies in Eastern Europe now. There's a lack of business skills, and revenue and profit will be different. Therefore, a firm line has to be drawn [between Colgate's East and West European organizations]." Bergin argues that although the business environment is in some senses "simpler" than in the West, "the risk of getting caught is greater."

Internal Pressures

Differential progress

Organizational theorists sometimes assume that sales and marketing operations in a number of different countries are all at roughly the same stage of development. The experience of the companies in this report indicates that this is seldom the case. Even if national operations are set up at the same time with the same product range and capital resources, the response of each market is likely to vary, the strength of competition will almost certainly vary, and the abilities of each management will definitely vary.

The result is differential growth, and thus varying demands on central management time and resources. In practice, most international networks spread outward a country or two at a time, initially often via a local distributor rather than a wholly owned subsidiary. In one country, too, one product may be the big profit earner before all others. In another, the order will be reversed, perhaps for market reasons, perhaps merely because of the personalities of the management. Some of these differences may average out, but they may also be incremental, and widen the gap between the most and the least successful product.

Heinz provides a clear example of a company that has grown differentially. As a result, the organization reflects four levels of development. Just two European countries, the UK and Italy (respectively, responsible also for Ireland, and for Spain and Portugal), account for 40% of the $2.4 billion sales outside the US. These operations therefore report direct to senior vice president, Europe, Paul Corddry, who divides his time between the US and the European regional office near London. A managing director, headquartered in Brussels and also reporting to Corddry, heads operations in Belgium, the Netherlands, France and Germany. An export general manager handles sales to Scandinavia and Switzerland, as well as the Middle East and Central and South America. A second general manager has recently been appointed to handle Central and Eastern Europe, and the Soviet Union, where a joint venture is being set up.

The effective organization thus has to be versatile enough at the very least to accommodate wide differences without strain, and at the most to assist the central management in its natural urge to bring the least developed markets up to the standard of the best. Companies have developed a number of ways of transmitting local excellence throughout a group. Most would admit that this process, though only just beginning, is being given increasing priority (see Chapter 7).

The demands of the product

It is vital that corporate structures keep pace with any changes in the marketing structure demanded by the products or the underlying technology. The Nixdorf and NCR examples (see Chapter 1) demonstrated the serious consequences of the business drifting away from the groups' rigid structures. Equally damaging is the allied risk that the structure does not allow new technologies the management focus and freedom they need to develop. The classic product divisions widely used to make the existing business manageable carry the attendant risk that promising developments that don't fit in could be frozen out.

This problem has given rise to a number of "intrapreneurial" techniques aimed at fostering and building new innovative businesses around the technology coming out of the central labs. The Swedish plastics group Perstorp is a keen advocate of such methods, which have accounted for much of its growth in recent years. The UK-based electronic instruments company Eurotherm, a world leader in many fields of temperature and process control, has grown steadily over the past 25 years in the face of competition from giants like Honeywell and Foxboro Yoxall. Crucial has been its policy of spinning off each promising new development into a separate subsidiary at the earliest practical moment, and relying on highly motivated and autonomous managers to build it into a worthwhile business alongside the others.

The rapid rate of technological change in certain industries like electronics, combined with the increasing investment demanded and shorter payback period, means that companies have to ensure that product breakthroughs are quickly and effectively exploited throughout the group. In the past, many companies have tightened the central control of their operations for this purpose. Now, the preferred course is to maintain local autonomy but increase the level of communication and intragroup cooperation to ensure willing, enthusiastic and imaginative support for new developments elsewhere.

Technological change does not always come in clearly labeled packets, however. As the following examples show, effective exploitation requires imaginative local application, and the organization to support it:

● **The chemical sector:** To help escape the slow growth and vulnerability to economic cycles of the commodity chemical business, many of the world industry leaders have concentrated on developing markets for specialty or effect chemicals, from dynamite to anaesthetics. But these products require much more sophisticated marketing and selling, and often close contact with the customer to develop solutions to his technical problems.

ICI, which now derives around half its turnover from effect chemicals, has recently begun a major program to make all its staff more aware of the marketing imperative. Further, to strengthen its hand in "solution marketing," it has bought several systems houses, small hi-tech firms specializing in solving technical problems in specific industries like shoe manufacture.

Du Pont has set up a number of marketing groups with executives drawn from different product divisions to focus on all of the chemical needs of a specific industry, such as autos or electronics. Du Pont also hopes that these groups will help overcome the traditional isolationism of the company's product divisions, and encourage the transfer of technology from, say, composites to fibers.

● **The computer sector:** Two separate technological developments have affected computer marketing profoundly in the past few years. First, the move down the size and unit value scale, while maintaining computing power, has meant the end of direct selling for the ubiquitous PCs, and a rising proportion of sales of all sizes of computers, even mainframes, through intermediaries. Second, open systems, particularly in Europe, are overtaking the proprietary software that so effectively kept customers loyal. With open systems, customers are free to choose the hardware and software from whichever manufacturer suits them.

IBM has therefore had to learn about serious marketing the hard way, and pushed 8,000 people out of national headquarters into branch offices to be nearer to customers. With the executives has gone a fair measure of authority and power: "The center of gravity of the business is going down," observes Elio Catania, IBM's vice president of market development in Europe.

The demands of the customer

A growing corporate preoccupation is meeting the multinational demands of customers. Chemicals, computers, copiers—all have a high proportion of users with operations in more than one country. Even in food products and toiletries, 8-10 international buying groups are already being formed with the prime purpose (in the manufacturers' view) of extracting ever larger discounts based on Europewide turnover.

One of the furthest developed is the **European Retail Alliance** (ERA), set up in 1989 by Argyll (the UK foods group that owns the UK grocery chain Safeway), the French supermarket chain Casino and the largest Dutch food retailer Ahold. ERA in turn owns 60% of Associated Marketing Services (AMS), headquartered in Zug, Switzerland, which is planning a joint label and common purchasing of major items like wine and petfood. The members of AMS, in addition to the three above, are Dansk Supermarked, ICA of Sweden, Kesko of Finland, La Rinascente of Italy, Mercadona of Spain, Migros of Switzerland and Allkauf of Germany. It is intended that suppliers of a particular product will pay AMS, say, 1% of their total sales to its members. In return, suppliers will be able to increase their sales of the product, and cut costs by, for example, all members agreeing on a common formulation for private label use.

Traditional geographical organizations where country managers are responsible for pricing are in obvious difficulty in cross-frontier negotiations. But even groups with strong international product divisions face problems when the negotiations extend across divisional boundaries. Depending on industry, the following areas can be affected:

- country managers' profit responsibilities;

- central and local manufacturing, and distribution facilities;

- ordering procedures and credit arrangements (in the grocery trade, the customary payment period ranges from 15 days to 120 days across European countries);

- aftersales service;

- management information systems.

The Swiss chemical/pharmaceutical company **Roche** clearly foresees the trend as it will affect its vitamins, flavors and fragrances product areas. With the help of the Boston Consulting Group, it is currently reexamining its whole corporate structure under executive committee member Markus Altwegg. He anticipates that the big food manufacturers could have one central buying operation for the whole of Europe within the next few years.

Altwegg believes that Roche will have to build Eurosales teams that deal with this one central organization. For such large customers, there will no longer be local teams in individual countries with the main marketing and sales responsibility. And as customers centralize, orders will become bigger, meaning that customers will have more sophisticated demands. Roche sales and marketing teams will have to develop a broader approach to satisfy a wider range of tastes.

Indicative of the way the "one-customer, one-price" trend is developing, in 1990 four European airlines—Swissair, SAS, Finnair and Austrian Airlines—jointly requested the European Airbus consortium and the US McDonnell Douglas to tender for up to 240 narrow-bodied twin-engined aircraft. The purpose was to obtain price reductions by agreeing a common specification.

MNCs' traditional response to the increasing single market awareness of customers has been to increase head office coordination. But companies are also firmly committed to lean head offices and decentralized power. Roche's stated intention is typical of many: "The local organization should have as much responsibility as possible to handle local business. We consider that a strength of Roche."

Partial solutions

In many industries, central purchasing is only just beginning to make itself felt, with many suppliers handling no more than a fraction of business in this way. There is a wide recognition that the organizational answers they have so far arrived at are only partially effective. How far companies have got in finding solutions is examined in the following chapters.

Chapter 3

The Role of the Center

The international development of a large company has always added as much complexity as it has sales and profits. Market conditions as well as customs, cultures, laws and economics can differ significantly from country to country, so the effective corporate structure must be versatile: it has to allow for all the differences, as well as capitalizing on them wherever possible; and it has to develop the similarities. Imposing a rigid formula may yield dividends in certain services like car hire or fast food where no local companies have yet built up custom and practice, but for the great majority of companies covered in this report, the key qualities aimed for are adaptation, flexibility, freedom of maneuver, combined with specific support such as "thought leadership" and "consultancy" (two of the definitions mentioned) as well as the inevitable pressure for results.

The Decline of the Large Head Office

In the early 1970s, head office authority was based on a theory (if managers stopped to think about it) that techniques like corporate planning, financial analysis and forecasting could secure the profitable growth of the business into the future, that futurology and scenario generation could shorten the odds on investment in new activities, and that staff functionaries could actively assist or direct the field battalions in developing the investment program. Four factors worked together to cut the head office pretensions down to size:

- **Unforeseen upsets:** Two oil crises and the following recessions demonstrated the dangers of too heavy a reliance on planning. More recently, the sudden and similarly unexpected collapse of communism in Central and Eastern Europe, and the crisis in the Gulf destroyed any lingering hopes that the future would yield to careful analysis.

- **Technological revolutions:** The development of new technologies, particularly electronics, has changed the way that companies conduct business. The only practical way to keep up with the trends has been to stay as close as possible to the market.

- **Portfolio management:** This popularized the advantage of selling off corporate problems rather than nursing them back to health, and buying in to add to existing strengths rather than relying on organic growth.

- **CEO assertiveness:** The chief executive officer has developed a closer, more direct relationship with the heads of business units rather than working through a large central staff. Sharing a vision becomes as important as the detail of the budget.

According to Tim Breene, consultant to WCRS, an international advertising agency (owned 60% by the French Eurocom group, 40% by the British Aegis), at senior management levels in multinationals "people are seeing more clearly the difference between leadership and central services." Figures like Mike Angus at the head of Unilever, Helmut Maucher at Nestlé, Anders Scharp at Electrolux, Percy Barnevik at Asea Brown Boveri and his rival Jack Welsh at the US General Electric have all assumed a much higher profile than some of their predecessors, have been instrumental in major acquisition programs, and often deal directly with the leaders of their business units rather than through armies of head office executives.

Corporate power is, in effect, being swept in two directions from under the feet of middle management: upward toward the chief executive and a handful of top executives, and downward to the heads of the operating units. The following examples illustrate the trend:

■ Within a week of taking over as chairman of **BP** in early 1990, Robert Horton announced that more than 1,000 jobs would be eliminated from its London headquarters. With them went some 70 corporate center committees and the whole hierarchical structure. "What I'm trying to do," he said, when announcing the changes, "is to simplify, refocus, make it clear that we don't need any longer to have hierarchies. We don't need any longer to have baronial head office departments. This is a fundamentally different way of looking at the way you run the center of the corporation." In place of hierarchy, he foresees, will be networks; in place of central control, real delegation. Horton expects the transformation to take two or three years; critics say four or five.

■ Also in early 1990, **Hoechst**, Germany's second-largest chemical company, was undergoing its biggest reorganization in 20 years. In the past, each of its 15 major product divisions had been run by a committee consisting of the heads of the product and functional subcommittees, chaired by a nonexecutive "first among equals." Now, a chief executive has been appointed for each division, responsible for a proportion of the 100 or so business units that have been set up with their own marketing, sales and other functional components. By the time the new structure is complete, much of the decision making will have been moved way from the center to the business units— some of them located outside Germany.

Keeping the Regional Office Down to Size

Pushing responsibility away from the center and nearer to the market is, in some instances, a step of only relative significance. A European regional head office in Geneva, Brussels or London can become a mushrooming center of corporate power in its turn. Many have been cut back, along with the global headquarters, but there is an opposite tendency for some to be set up from scratch or to grow further as the trend toward coordinating European marketing and sales accelerates.

All of the companies in this report based outside Europe maintain European regional offices, and the rationale is plain. Distance and the size of individual markets, the continuing need to

---

THE CENTER AS RESOURCE, NOT DICTATOR

A new awareness is developing in some companies that it is up to the country managers and others to pull out of the center the resources they need, rather than have the center dictate their requirements for them. This has long been standard for justifying capital investments. Not so common is the extension of the principle to technical, marketing and sales support. However, there are good reasons for doing so:

- Subsidiaries are much more likely to use resources effectively if they can call for the support themselves rather than have it thrust down their throats.

- Poor performance cannot then be blamed on inappropriate central policies.

---

consider and manage each one separately, and cultural factors usually dictate that a regional office be set up as:

- a focus for the national subsidiaries to ensure that their views and preferences are given due weight by the company's central management;

- a performance monitor, to check what results should be expected from each subsidiary;

- an interpreter of central direction as it affects subsidiary managements;

- a vehicle for managing whatever is pan-European about the product—technical specifications, packaging, advertising, servicing multinational customers, liaison with the EC, as well as finance, manufacturing and research;

- a vehicle for joint ventures and acquisitions, and a base for operations in Eastern Europe.

Most regional heads have specific profit responsibility with country managers reporting direct to them, but their degree of independence from the global headquarters and the extent of their involvement with the marketing and sales of the national companies vary widely. While IBM in Paris (like Rank Xerox near London) is sharply curtailing the activities of its large regional office, Levi Strauss, with a small unit in Brussels, shoulders half the marketing burden for its European operations. Procter & Gamble's 600 staff in Brussels (including technicians) appear to be growing in influence, but such a large regional office may become a rarity as better ways are found of coordinating and dispersing marketing operations.

Some MNCs find it advantageous to extend the central authority through the regional head office. The troubled **Union Carbide**, for instance, recently reshaped itself into a holding company with three main worldwide product divisions—carbon products, gases, and chemicals and plastics. All three now operate their own sales subsidiaries in the main national European markets (some are still being established) to facilitate the process of acquisition and divestment. But the three all center their European operations firmly on Geneva, where business directors conduct the marketing, set the prices and select the source of their products for the whole of Europe. Country managers are left to build relationships with client companies according to plans laid down in Geneva. European sales of Union Carbide's chemicals and plastics increased by 25% in 1989.

The Japanese approach

Japanese companies are different again. While most large ones have now set up regional European offices, their role is often to discuss, advise and encourage rather than to exert formal profit supervision. Panasonic evidently still has some way to go in weaning its regional office away from Tokyo's influence over detail: its brochure explaining its European structure and the autonomy it enjoys from Osaka is nevertheless printed in Japan—with several typographical and stylistic mistakes. But generally, Japanese companies leave their subsidiaries to run their own businesses.

☞ Freeing the subsidiary at Canon

Japanese electronics company Canon does not interpose regional authority between the larger European subsidiaries and Tokyo. The president of Canon Europa, Takeshi Mitarai, explains his role: "The Big Three subsidiaries (France, Germany and the UK) report their daily activities on sales, purchasing, price negotiations etc. direct to Tokyo, but their profit is reported to me. I report to the president for sales, profits and finance . . . Generally speaking, they run their own businesses—I just check the monthly financial data." The smaller operations do report to Mitarai, and "many times, I ask them, 'please keep more profitable'"—indicating a light, supervisory hand on the controls. Some five years ago, the Big Three reported through the Europa office, but the inefficiency involved in shipping products to Europe led to the present ambiguous system—untidy by US standards, but effective. In Tokyo, the reporting lines are simply not a big issue, and as one Canon main board director remarked a few years ago, "We're quite flexible. We have a permanent employment system, and we know each other very well, so we do not need formal channels."

Many Japanese companies are intent on building up their manufacturing facilities in Europe, as are US companies, to avoid being locked out of "Fortress Europe," and the regional head office is a convenient point at which to focus responsibility, either complete or partial, for European production. Canon, for example, has factories in Germany and France, and a small research center in the UK, all placed with an eye to the political impact. More generally, factories in the past were frequently under the control of the country managers, and supplied little more than one or two national markets. But the case for rationalizing European production has long been more clear-cut than for marketing and sales, and the lowering of barriers will hasten the process, ensuring a continuing role for the regional head office.

The European response

Interestingly, even European companies are coming to find a separate European regional office an advantage. **ICI** has long had its Europa operation based in Brussels, while Unilever and BP have announced that they are following suit. In ICI's case, the original aim was to focus the UK-based product divisions' attentions on prospects in continental markets, but now, for all of them, the regional office is intended to ensure that the European customer's viewpoint is given more weight at the center, and to prevent too much central influence and thinking from biasing national subsidiaries' judgment and stunting their development. All three are aware that even if central and regional managements, on the same site, are separated by brick walls as well as lines on the organization chart, influence penetrates by osmosis, and local managers in Madrid or Milan will always assume that regional and central managements are as one.

The Purpose of Central Control

> "We maintain a small staff at the center in Britain which acts on occasion as traffic policeman, sometimes as an orchestra conductor, infrequently as an auditor, and very often as a cheer leader."
>
> Richard Giordano, chairman, BOC, to the London Business School.

Much has been written about the varying roles played by the central authority in companies. Whether or not it adds value to the business units it controls is a question about which, to say the least, employees are likely to have strong and often uncomplimentary views. Descriptions of the head office as "galactic HQ," "the bunker" or "the Kremlin" are not uncommon. The implied criticism often remains valid: the central authority, whether in the corporate headquarters or in a European regional head office, is too often seen as remote and formidable. It needs to understand, and to communicate to others, how it adds to the corporate wealth and avoids obstructing others in the process.

There is one overwhelming reason: the key local executives in international businesses are peculiarly vulnerable to the feeling of alienation from the center. They have to be part of the team, yet they are inevitably apart and different, and they face different challenges and problems. They need to be entrepreneurial in fighting local competition, figureheads in the local community, but good company men when dealing with corporate matters. They are therefore likely to feel insecure and to take a critical interest in head office policies and method of working—and to resist any infringement of their territory.

It follows that the central authority should be consistent and open in its relationship with local executives. But companies have expressed greatly differing opinions on how to achieve this. Some, like **American Express** and the UK engineering groups **TI Group** and **GKN**, took a certain pride in having "very, very clear lines of authority," as one put it. A similar culture existed in some other organizations, laid down in uniform, clear-cut organization charts: one commented that its managers well understood that "should you wish not to work in this environment, you should do something else."

In contrast, **Electrolux, Canon, ICI** and **Nestlé** (equally, if not more successful) all prefer fuzzier relationships, acknowledging that people and the demands of business do not always fit into neat organizational boxes, and that the overriding aim is effective operation and speed of reaction rather than logical uniformity. ICI's chairman, Denys Henderson, sums up this approach: "The structure lacks clarity, but then we're in a complex industry. We hope that most arguments can be sorted out by discussion."*

---

* *Financial Times*, August 9, 1989.

One recent attempt to clarify the roles that companies adopt at the center in relation to their portfolio of businesses has been developed by Andrew Campbell and Michael Goold of the Ashridge Strategic Management Centre working in conjunction with McKinsey's London office. They distinguish three separate "parenting" roles:

- **The Controller** adds value by picking the right managers and motivating them effectively with financial targets.

- **The Coach** uses its knowledge and experience of each business to develop and build strategy, judge and improve operating performance, and share skills and best practice (e.g. Unilever).

- **The Orchestrator** coordinates a chain of businesses to realize the synergies available from marketing and manufacturing (e.g. IBM).

Many companies, taken as wholes, fall into either the coaching or the orchestrating categories. But the range of their activities, the stages of development of each subsidiary, the personalities of the individuals, the state of design and manufacturing technology, and the degree of competition in a given market ensure that they have to use all patterns selectively for different markets at different times.

Electrolux, whose products range from refrigerators, through earth-moving equipment to plastic flowers, describes itself openly as "an impossible organization, but the only one that will work." According to one top executive, its group president and chief executive Anders Scharp "acts as an orchestrator toward white goods, as a coach toward Gränges (the aluminum subsidiary) and as a controller toward agricultural machinery."*

Still, if the classification helps to clarify the actual relationship between the center and its operating units, and to implant in managers' minds the knowledge that there are different modes of operation that the central authority can adopt, and that the present one is not necessarily the most appropriate, it will have performed a valuable service.

Key Central Functions

According to the executives interviewed for this report, of the many functions performed by the center in respect of the sales and marketing operations, the following are the most important:

- defining the strategy;

- supplying the means;

- appointing the right executives;

- ensuring best practice; and

- monitoring performance.

---

* *Financial Times*, June 19, 1989.

Defining the strategy

This involves answering the strategic question, "What business are we in?" and following the logic of the answer. The process of leadership starts with a vision of some distant and desirable objective, and communicating the enthusiasm for it to the whole group. For many companies contemplating future global, not just European, competition, this has meant abandoning earlier attempts to be strong in many product and service areas in a few geographical markets, in favor of strength in a few products in the majority of markets.

The UK-based **TI Group** sold out of bicycles and domestic appliances, among other activities, and concentrated on industrial seals for machinery and hi-tech tubing, markets in which it was already strong and now has leading world shares. It had only 2.5% of the world market for domestic appliances. TI's chairman and chief executive Chris Lewinton argues, "We either had to sell everything and go into apppliances, or sell appliances." TI chose the latter, leaving Electrolux and the US Whirlpool as the top two white goods manufacturers in the world.

For many companies, this process of consolidation still has a long way to run. Electrolux itself, for example, is likely to hive off some of its more peripheral activities in the near future. But equally important is the need for the central management to spot the weaknesses in whatever it decides are its core products, as well as to take advantage of any suitable opportunities that arise. Acquisition is a natural way of rectifying the imbalance.

Supplying the means

Securing a constant flow of new products, technologies or applications to the field is a central office priority. Transferring knowhow from one part of the group to another, setting aside sufficient R&D funds and directing them to the most promising projects, or buying in the relevant expertise (and selling off the irrelevant) can be secured only with energy and funds from the center. The allocation of resources, whether for the development of new products and markets, or the defense of existing ones, is, of course, an integral part of all of these activities.

Paul Girolami, chairman of the UK pharmaceutical group Glaxo, explained his own board's policies in a paper given some years ago to the London School of Economics. Since the group has become the fourth-largest drugs company, having developed the world's top selling pharmaceutical, Zantac, worries have grown about its geographical spread and about what will replace the product that still accounts for more than half of group profits. Girolami told his audience:

> It has been the object of policy in recent years to correct this imbalance: by entering those markets in which the group was absent; by strengthening the companies in those markets where its presence was weak; by entering into joint marketing arrangements; and finally by adopting a change from "production push through" to a new "marketing pull through." One result of these steps is that the marketing resources in the next five years could become powerful enough to create the need for more products than even our considerable research and development resources could be reasonably expected to supply. With this in mind, a new department has recently been established actively to seek new products from other concerns. Moreover, joint venture and co-marketing arrangements have, as a

secondary objective, the establishment of relationships which could improve the chances of getting products from outside.

Companies in the business-to-business markets such as Rank Xerox, Honeywell, the computer companies, and the specialty end of chemicals are more inclined to provide the products centrally, and leave the adaptation of them and application to customers' specific needs at the local level so that they can provide a close and effective service. But for consumer markets, where common brand positioning and messages are more important, the initiative, if not the ideas, can come only from the center.

Moulinex, the French manufacturer of small domestic electric appliances, was, until a management buyout in 1987, heavily centralized and in decline. The new management team has set up a product/country matrix, with the center retaining a minimum of functions, including product policy and positioning. Group sales director Gilbert Torelli explains: "We have kept a central group function for design and packaging. This is important as we still have to have a coherent Moulinex identity. In advertising, too, I think that we are going to have to think more about coherence . . . It's up to me to say that by 1992–93 we need to have at least a common claim for the group. We all need to say the same thing. The brand name should be European, with the same claim everywhere."

☞ Managing the argument at Lego

Danish toy manufacturer Lego, one of the 10 largest toy manufacturers in the world, sells an identical range of interlocking plastic bricks in 125 countries round the world. It is also fortunate that its product is almost uniquely noncultural—while parental attitudes may differ, children will use it in much the same way. Lego has a regional head office for the 14 European sales companies, where as many of the management functions as possible are concentrated. Christian Majgaard, European marketing vice president, explains the corporate policy:

> Let's be honest, we are a fairly centralized company. That's always been the case, and I don't see any trend toward greater decentralization in the 1990s. One problem I can see is that for many reasons we do have, and I think we will still have in the 1990s, an international, not even European product development. I also think that for many reasons we will have a European marketing strategy and a European advertising fund in 80% of instances, with the remaining 20% hopefully coming from the countries. What I think will happen is that because there might be other reasons for centralizing certain functions (you may have different logistic structures in the 1990s), we should nurture more carefully aspects of management that can be decentralized, simply because we might end up having a too demotivated national management. That's a danger.

Lego professes a management philosophy called "the philosophy of the argument," forbidding headquarters personnel to order local managers to take a particular action: "We want to be able to convince, and if we can't convince, then maybe we don't have a case." By all accounts, Lego had to learn the hard way. According to Kamran Kashani, professor of marketing at the International Institute for Management Development in Lausanne, Lego suffered a massive loss of market share in the US when a rival selling a similar product began putting its bricks in plastic buckets, useful for storing them after play. The idea was popular, and Lego's US managers asked permission to follow suit. The Danish HQ, anxious to maintain its uniform cardboard packs round the world, turned down the proposal, only to reverse its decision two years later when the damage was apparent.

Appointing the right executives

Finding the right executives to run the group's operations is of vital importance, and for companies that are aiming for a compromise between centralized and decentralized structures (i.e. most of them), everything depends on this choice. As Colgate-Palmolive's European president Brian Bergin points out: "In setting up this sort of structure (for both global and local brands), you have to have first-class people who can think through a complex matrix-type decision process at the same time as dealing with a market in evolution."

Moving away from semi-independent companies to a more integrated structure has meant widespread management changes for a number of companies. Roger Thomas, European head of power tool manufacturer **Black & Decker**, recalls that "strong local fiefdoms" frustrated attempts in the early 1980s to draw the national European subsidiaries together. With competition building up, the central decision was made to force the changes—for example, the number of factories was reduced from 14 to three (plus two smaller sites). "But a change in the marketing culture (toward closer cooperation, but not centralization) required a change of management—I tried to keep the good people and change them, but I couldn't." In the end, "every single general manager and marketing manager in Europe was changed, apart only from the UK, Spain and Portugal."

Comments from other companies suggest that Black & Decker's experience is not unusual: changing systems and structures is comparatively easy; the difficult bit is changing the way people think and work. That is a process that can emanate only from the center, and, as Glaxo's Girolami insists, if it doesn't work, there is only one course: "a decision you don't delegate—you kick him out."

The US **Scott Paper** had a similar experience in its European development program. The company has been investing some $250 million in new paper machines in France, Italy and Spain. Although transport costs favor local distribution, the huge output from these machines demands that, at least initially, some must be sold across borders. The group therefore needed a pan-European structure. Jack Butler was brought over from the group's Pacific region to head the European operation, where he found that one of his key European managing directors was "not really prepared to manage in a pan-European context," which implied some loss of personal authority in his own country but wider responsibilities for (and longer hours visiting) other European operations. He left. Now, Butler has three managing directors reporting to him—the UK, Belgium/France and Italy/Spain/Portugal—and the program is going ahead according to plan.

Ensuring best practice

Increasing numbers of companies have decided to abandon the assumption that the center can supply from its own resources the necessary expertise to improve the operating units' performance. That role may have some value in a startup phase or in the introductory program for a radically new product, but many mature companies have found that the authoritarian route generally does not work. The central staff are too far removed from the customers, and impractical policies damage the center's reputation among subsidiaries. Instead, companies are selecting and propagating the ideas developed by their subsidiaries, a method they find to be cheaper and more effective.

☞ Cutting back the center at Rank Xerox

Rank Xerox aimed for a decade to develop local autonomy and responsibility, but the head office just kept on growing, producing what European marketing director Lyndon Haddon describes as "the strange strategies generated within the staff group." One Rank Xerox veteran adds: "The central organization tends to be filled with well-motivated smart executives who do what look like intelligent things. The trouble is, it's difficult to know what the group would be like without them."

The company maintained a staff of around 1,100 executives in the European head office outside London at its peak (reporting to the Xerox headquarters in the US), 250–300 of them in marketing and planning. Now, the marketing staff numbers no more than 20, but with a far bigger product range to cope with. Little has been lost, considers Haddon, because the operating companies "ignored the head office strategies anyway, and every time you put people in the chain, you got further and further away from your customers." Now, his main job has a more modest aim: "to ensure communication of best practice, and to provide advice, counsel, plus some pushing, to ensure the subsidiaries make their revenue plans."

☞ Doubting central control

Jean-Pierre Rosso, president of **Honeywell Europe**, makes the same point from his office in Brussels: "I have grave doubts about headquarters expertise. The only knowledge or expertise here is on legal, fiscal, financial issues etc." Honeywell has an evenly balanced matrix between, on the one axis, its business units ranging from domestic control systems to industrial and aerospace controls, and on the other, its country managers. But "if we impose a strategy, then we have problems. We spend a lot of time on 'ownership' of strategy. If the strategy process that links the business and affiliate together has been well done, people will do their best—they're buying it in."

By limiting central interference to identifying best practice among the subsidiaries, and disseminating this round the group, companies can ensure that the practices come ready field-tested. It also cuts overheads. (The implications are discussed more fully in Chapters 7 and 10.)

Monitoring performance

Many current trends, such as tougher, worldwide competition and shorter product lives, throw more strain on the center's ability to keep itself informed of market trends and to assess the performance of its operating units. Every budget and target implies a judgment as to what is possible, and therefore knowledge of the local conditions.

The large, centralized head office implies that executives there can make an intelligent assessment of, among other things:

HOW TO JUDGE LOCAL PERFORMANCE

- **Osram,** the German lighting division of the giant Siemens and third largest in the world, has "an ambitious but realistic" overall plan for realizing sales growth and other corporate goals, and it is applied to the national subsidiaries in a dialogue between HQ and each subsidiary.

- **Electrolux,** in spite of its informal, decentralized organization, believes in setting its managers tough, very detailed targets. The head of a UK stove factory recently described what it felt like to be taken over by the Swedish giant: "Half a dozen targets were handed out on one day. My first reaction was 'we can't achieve that much'—they involved a halving of fault rates in two years, a trebling of stockturn in 18 months and so on. I told the Electrolux people it was an impossible task, but they said 'we know it's feasible because we've done it elsewhere.'" They were right, and went on to invest £25 million in the plant.

- **L'Oréal,** the French hair care and cosmetics house and one of the leaders in the world market, controls its product development, packaging and advertising programs centrally, but devolves other aspects of marketing and sales to national subsidiaries. Sales targets are not set centrally. Says Giles Roger, assistant director for consumer products: "The desire to sell more is not handed down from the president telling his employees to do so; it comes from wanting to make and sell performance products—that's really company consensus. From the moment a product is ready for launch, there is a will to sell and sell more. But we develop products to be excellent, not to satisfy figures—everyone in the company agrees. Always trying to fulfill targets could even hamper our performance."

- To keep track of all of its 60,000 products, **3M** has set up some 40 European management action teams (Emats—see Chapter 7) covering the main product areas and consisting of representatives from the subsidiaries, from manufacturing etc. The Emats are the repositories of expertise on the products and their markets, and, it is claimed, enable the center to make an informed opinion about the performance of a particular subsidiary in a particular market.

- what growth a business unit should be achieving—20% a year may sound impressive at the shareholders' meeting, but may be sluggish if the market is growing at 50%;

- the local manager's explanation as to why he has fallen behind budget, his remedial action and the value of his predictions for the rest of the period;

- the strength of local competition (including incidence of predatory pricing);

- how the market differs from others;

- the general economic and social trends.

Large quantities of background data and analysis are therefore frequently required, with a high risk that the center will nevertheless miss the really significant underlying trends, or that the familiar "paralysis by analysis" will set in.

The entrepreneur's method of relying on personal judgment, or even the cruder "squeezing till the pips squeak," can sometimes produce spectacular results, at least in the short term, and is the basis of many conglomerates' success. The implications for the long-term health of the operation or for its wider international strategy may not be so favorable, however.

Developing the organization

Companies in their development phase are perhaps more vulnerable to the effects of poor organizational development than are more mature ones. The conventional progression of an entrepreneurial company from a domestic operation with some export sales to one with an export division (which still has to compete for attention with the domestic side), thence to overseas operations standing on their own feet but still on the group's periphery, and ultimately to a small holding company to which overseas and domestic operations report on an equal footing, rarely proceeds at the optimal pace for the development of the business. Changes are more often forced upon a reluctant group either by outside pressures or a new broom at the top. Critics have pointed out that Eastman Kodak, for example, was still, in the late 1970s, an essentially US domestic company with some overseas operations.

US-based **Compaq** Computer, in contrast, took just eight years to grow from zero to $3 billion sales. Compaq's president and CEO, Joseph Canion, decided from the outset that the company would be international in ambition and style. He appointed a German national, Eckhard Pfeiffer (they had been at Texas Instruments together), to set up the Compaq worldwide operation, which he did in Munich, 18 months after Compaq's foundation. "I'd seen the benefits of operating worldwide rather than having a strong home base with a little bit in other countries," he comments. Nearly half of Compaq's sales are now made outside the US, and the group is enjoying the benefit of a faster-growing market in its main desktop computer product lines.

The crucial feature in the Compaq structure is that Pfeiffer reports directly to Canion, so that the power and status given to the international operation are more or less equal to that accorded to the domestic one, and its development has not been subordinated to the needs of the home market. A consensus management style has also ensured that on issues like product development and specification, the worldwide market requirements are given due weight.

Achieving the balance

An effective balance between the center and the periphery is difficult to achieve. And it will shift with the pressure of events and with changing personalities. Inevitably, too, the reality may differ widely from the theory and the intention. In the following chapters, we examine the role of the country and product managers, and how they are being meshed together.

Part II
Europe and the Marketing Matrix

Chapter 4

The Objectives of European Organization

Designing a marketing organization for a complex entity like Europe demands a crystal clear understanding of the strategy it is designed to implement. Changing market conditions, profitability, maneuverability and productivity must all be taken into consideration and reflected in the grand design. The EC's 1992 program has provided a valuable stimulus to companies thinking about the way they organize their European operations, but there is a danger that managements will be tempted into the assumption that a regimented and coordinated pan-European organization is necessary for long-term profitable growth.

All the companies in this survey are operating in 15 or more European countries, selling anything from a handful of products to thousands. The organizational complexity that the number of permutations implies serves as a powerful warning against placing too heavy demands on the European structure. The need to control, coordinate and actively manage the European structure, whatever its shape, springs from any or all of the following:

- the limited ability or experience of the local management;

- the need to maximize returns from R&D and product ideas;

- the economies of scale derived from large-scale manufacturing and distribution;

- the cumulative strength of international branding;

- utilization of the available management talent and ideas;

- serving international customers;

- the economies of centrally produced advertising and international advertising media;

- the increasing speed needed to exploit innovations across markets before rivals seize the initiative.

Classic Corporate Structures

For companies where none of these factors is important enough to justify the expense and rigidities of a European organization, the basic financial controls, allowing maximum autonomy and scope for entrepreneurial initiative, may be the most appropriate for their strategic purposes. However, all of the companies in this study consider that some or all of these

ARE THE JAPANESE BETTER ORGANIZED?

A 1986 study conducted by Peter Doyle, professor of marketing at Warwick University in the UK, found that of 45 subsidiaries operating in the UK of US, Japanese and UK parents, the Japanese subsidiaries were more successful than their rivals in similar markets (and often run by UK managers with similar backgrounds) because:

+ they were more autonomous, but subject to often daily, informal monitoring rather than a formal control system;

+ reporting was concerned with the whole product-market situation: "The overriding financial focus of top management in American and British companies appeared to be a key reason for the lack of well-thought-out marketing strategies in their business, and their consequent disappointing performance in the market";

+ organizations were structured around individual products and geographical markets;

+ the Japanese subsidiaries were better at differentiating the segments of their market and targeting each one specifically.

Doyle also found that "47% of British and 40% of US companies (vs 13% of the Japanese) acknowledged that they were unclear about the main type of customers in the market and what their needs were." Another problem in the case of the US subsidiaries was that marketing decisions were often made by European or international committees outside the UK, and with little effort being made to differentiate among the European countries. "Thus when the Japanese concentrated their marketing investments on the high-potential customer groups in the UK, the British and Americans tended to spread theirs thinly across the entire market," concluded Doyle.

If globalization is allowed to imply as little discrimination between segments as Doyle's research suggests, it becomes a top-down, production-led process at odds with the marketer's local instincts.

factors demand closer management of their European structures and use one or more of the classic organizational patterns outlined below.

● **Functional divisions:** Here, R&D, manufacturing, marketing and selling are separated. Companies like IBM and SKF have relied upon this format in the past. They may make economic management of development and production simpler, but they obscure the profit or loss made by a given product in a particular market, and have long been discredited by theorists. Other studies have found that they are still very common, however.

● **Product divisions:** These may similarly obscure the performance of a particular market, as well as suffering from the parallel overheads of separate sales forces and administrative offices. But for large groups with capital-intensive production, like chemicals or automotive products, they are probably the only manageable units (see Chapter 6).

- **Geographical divisions:** Geographically based sales and marketing structures, with or without their own manufacturing facilities, are by far the most common form in this survey. But they lack the mechanisms of their own to spawn international products or to rationalize sales and marketing expenditure across all European markets—let alone round the globe (see Chapter 5).

- **Matrix structures:** These are intended to rationalize the inherent conflicts between any two of the above (normally product and country divisions). Regarded as inevitable in some companies and giving organizational expression to inherent conflicts, they add to the administrative burden, and tend to spread management attention evenly rather than concentrate it on specific nodes. For others, the expense and loss of entrepreneurial freedom implicit in a matrix structure are not worth the foreseeable advantages: "We hate matrices" and "They are regarded like leprosy" are two representative comments.

- **Matrix plus:** A number of companies have reacted to intensifying competition with a variety of tactical adjustments. 3M, for instance, has introduced European management action teams, while Unilever has developed European brand groups (see Chapter 7).

The models mentioned above are only starting points. Their shortcomings—adding complexity, exacerbating power struggles, slowing up the decision-making process etc.—have prompted many companies to devise both formal and informal ways of compensating for them. For many others, the bureaucracy thus created is simply not worth the possible benefits.

Reorganizing for a Changed Market

Companies that persist with an organization long after the conditions for which it was originally designed have changed are courting disaster. A number of companies in the present survey have reorganized themselves specifically to reflect changing circumstances and new priorities.

☞ **Radical change at Levi Strauss**

Radical change was required at jeans manufacturer Levi Strauss to bring the organization into line with strategy. Having expanded too far and too fast in the early 1980s while its core jeans product remained static, the company was heading for serious trouble when the new president Robert D Haas (a descendent of the original Levi Strauss) conducted a $1.6 billion buyout from the controlling shareholders in 1984. According to the new director of marketing services in Europe, John Ankeny, the company decided that the only way to restore margins was to leave country managers responsible for profit on (a reduced) sales volume, but to centralize marketing, advertising etc. in a 20-strong marketing team in the Brussels regional office.

The central team is responsible for product merchandising as well as marketing, and there is a centrally managed manufacturing program for core products (like its 501 range of jeans). The degree of computer control is increasingly sophisticated. Country managers specify the quantities, colors, sizes etc., but are free to add to the range from their own sources (mainly tops). They are then responsible for selling the mix of global and local product lines to a carefully selected network of nominated retailers. Speed of reaction and close cooperation with the retail trade is vital in an increasingly fickle, fashion-conscious market. "There's no way we could make a sensible decision on the local market," says Ankeny, "but when you combine the volumes and margins, you've got enough money to spend on TV advertising. We're in an image business."

The changes were not popular with some country managers, most of whom were replaced for that and other reasons. Levi Strauss is now riding high once more, claiming around 12% of the European market and "60–70% of the niche in which we compete."

Reorganizing for Profit

A significant number of companies in this survey have listed increased profit as a reason for organizational change. Even IBM intends that its new decentralized structure will help its staff focus on profit rather than volume, and country managers now have to "buy in" central marketing support services to ensure the overheads are justified. It is important to recognize the specific mechanisms that can impede or assist profit growth.

☞ Renault's cultural shift

Renault Automobiles, part of the French state-owned automotive group Régie Renault, places design and manufacture under a senior technical director. Sales and marketing (and the country-based sales companies) head up to a theoretically equal-ranking sales director, and pricing is the ultimate responsibility of the finance department. Heavy losses in the early 1980s convinced the management that the old product-oriented methods were too cumbersome for modern markets, and closer liaison between factory and field was necessary to cut inventories, speed customer response etc. Some 90% of output is now manufactured to order.

The overall goal has been to push the group back into profit, but that has not yet been achieved. The functional structure has been retained, but a horizontal, project management system for the development of individual models has been instituted to help break down internal barriers. One principal effect of these and other changes has been a cultural shift among executives, says Claude Lancelle, director of commercial planning. "We talk about money; people are aware that the company has to generate profits, and that everyone has a contribution to make."

☞ Achieving profit awareness at SKF

Until three years ago, SKF was, like Renault, largely organized by function. The marketing director for what is now SKF Bearing Industries, Anders Braennstroem, explains that as a result of the restructuring, "what is important is that you have profitability awareness and focus on a much lower (downstream) level in the organization than before." The group's bearing interests were previously split between the large parent company in Sweden, AB SKF, and similar composite companies in North America, the rest of Europe and elsewhere. They were functionally organized so that "the only profit center was the company."

The bearing business is naturally divided not only by product type, but between sales to the original equipment manufacturers and the after-market. As with chemicals, there is also a big difference between commodity customers, and those requiring a specialized technical service and product. The bearing interests were therefore reformed into five worldwide product divisions, one of them for the after-market, one covering the volume bearing business. The latter has been further divided by business line, and a matrix structure set up with a central marketing function and country managers. Each business line and each country is now a separate profit center, and "today, line managers are much more responsible for the bottom line." SKF ascribes much of its 63% profit increase in 1989 to this new awareness.

☞ Transferring experience in Colgate-Palmolive

"One of the real 1992 challenges," says Brian Bergin, European president of Colgate-Palmolive (C-P), "will be 'Did you lift your profits well compared to your competitors, and take the opportunity to get ahead of them?'" Apart from rationalizing manufacture and logistics, increasing profitability means building on the brands that are, or have the potential to be, Europewide because they tend to be more profitable and have the capacity to grow. But Bergin notes, "The difficulty is to ensure that in focusing on the global products you don't lose profitability on the local ones." C-P has always been "geographically propelled," and CEO Reuben Mark has encouraged a fresh spirit of independence and entrepreneurship.

Not all of the details of Bergin's solution have been revealed yet, but a regional company, Colgate Europe, is already in place, charged with developing a single manufacturing network, and providing the base for profit-responsible general managers for the four core categories of product. These cut across the country managers' responsibilities, and Bergin admits to "a number of healthy arguments—but you've got to go through it." He is determined not to build a big edifice in Brussels—a staff of 50 at the most—and the category managers' support staff may well be located in one or other of the national companies. "The category has only one purpose—the transfer of experience." The speed at which it can do that across frontiers will determine long-term success: "If a company isn't fast enough, rivals will use its idea somewhere else." Structural changes throughout the C-P group have helped to give the company seven years of volume growth, and it has already comfortably exceeded its target of a 5% aftertax return by 1991, set when Mark became CEO in 1984.

Reorganizing for Brand Advantage

Some consultants see a danger in consumer goods companies pursuing international brand harmonization—and organization structures to match—for benefits that will prove illusory. John Hegarty of London consultants Brand Positioning Services, a Unilever breakaway, believes managements should be clear what it is they are trying to standardize internationally, and why:

> Is the objective standard production, for example, in one or two factories supplying a whole continent? Or is it rather brand values and their communication in media advertising? It can be important not to confuse the two: major economies may be possible by bringing into line the ingredients/components and formulations/specifications of products manufactured centrally, even though they may be sold under different brand names and with different consumer propositions in different countries . . . Conversely, a single international brand proposition may be delivered successfully in different coun-

tries by local formulations produced in local factories to suit local tastes, using a single international advertising campaign. Too much international marketing seeks standardization for standardization's sake, without a sufficiently clear analysis and definition of the commercial benefits being sought. It is vital to decide why, and therefore what, you want to internationalize.

This decision process is especially troublesome for large companies with a long list of brands. "Who decides whether they are different or not?" asks Howard Belton, the senior marketing member of Unilever's Detergent Coordination. Belton is emphatic that "if you try to impose uniformity, you suboptimize." The essential issue for an old Unilever detergent brand like Omo, sold in a number of countries, is not one of product specification but one of positioning in each market, different for historical reasons. Making it an effective international brand therefore requires it to be levered slowly into some common position, which will certainly be expensive and could in some instances turn out to be impractical.

Lever Europe, Unilever's soaps and detergents division, has categorized its brands into three groups:

- established international brands like the modern Jif cleaner and the original, 100-year-old Sunlight soap;

- local brands; and

- convergence brands—these could become international at some point in the future.

But the predominantly geographical organization that has characterized Unilever's growth is not well adapted to applying the pressure needed to move convergence brands into the international category, and over a decade or more, the European structure has been steadily adapted to meet the new demands in a process of continual evolution. Its latest changes and structure are explained in Chapter 7.

Other companies have adopted different classifications, but the purpose is the same.

United Distillers, the reorganized Johnnie Walker whisky and Gordon's gin offshoot of the Guinness group, has had to classify its more than 50 brands by position and geographical market prior to concentrating its resources on the brand/markets with the greatest potential and introducing some order into its international marketing.

Before deciding to sell the Swiss chocolate and coffee firm Jacobs Suchard to US tobacco company Philip Morris, chairman and CEO Klaus Jacobs divided Suchard's brands into global, core local and "local excitements." Jacobs' purpose was "to discriminate more clearly among them in the longer-term balance we have to strike between local entrepreneurism and central coordination."*

Companies with a more centralized culture and history may find the harmonization process simpler, but they can still experience problems.

---

* McKinsey Quarterly, winter 1987.

PROCTER & GAMBLE'S CATEGORY MANAGERS

In order to move faster and more cohesively in Europe, Procter & Gamble (P&G) has introduced senior category managers covering product groups such as detergents, fabric conditioners, beverages and disposables etc. in major countries, who bring together manufacturing and sales as well as marketing and advertising. These executives, with or without a lead country role, report in a matrix structure to both the national manager and the geographical divisional managers, who also carry Europewide responsibility for a product category. As well as providing a formal European dimension to product management, observers point out that the category managers bring profit responsibility closer to the market, and should prevent the internecine warfare between individual brands that characterized the traditional P&G brand management structure. The structure, excluding personal care and paper products (like Pampers), is illustrated below in simplified form.

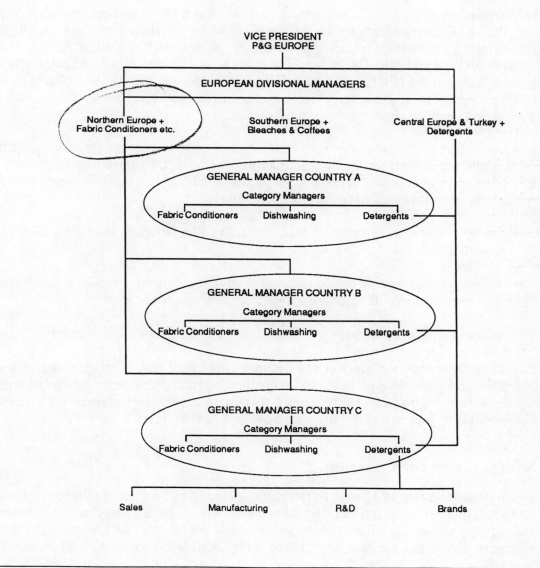

Reorganizing for Maneuverability

Whatever the group decides its stance in European markets should be, it must be prepared to change tack rapidly to meet altered circumstances. As one executive remarked, "If you read about it, it's too late." The environmental challenge is just one issue that has demanded a rapid response from detergent manufacturers, for example, with the action matched to differing levels of concern in the various European countries.

Companies also have to increase the flow of new models onto the market, cutting development time. 3M's vice president for its European marketing subsidiaries, Edoardo Pieruzzi, says that for the company's prolific new product program, it has now adopted a "planned roll-out approach—but we'll have to get faster." For Colin Brown, group director in charge of European household and toiletry products at Reckitt & Colman, selling in Europe's different markets means that "unless you're coordinated, you'll be late somewhere."

This does not imply a large coordinating staff, however. "We run Europe with four people," says Brown. Country managers are left firmly in charge of their own markets, but when the group finds a successful product anywhere that has potential in a wider market, it is rolled out as quickly as possible. One example was the Magic Mushroom, an Airwick air freshener that originated in the US. It was successfully introduced into the UK, and then launched onto 14 other European markets in 18 months, each one requiring some element of national difference as well as international harmonization.

It is significant that most companies find the coordination process for new products much quicker and easier than for the old-established ones, and companies like 3M, which expects 25% of its sales in any year to come from products that are less than five years old, score for that reason. New products have the advantages that:

- the technical requirements of each market can be designed into the product from the outset;

- the market positioning can be planned in advance, therefore avoiding many harmonization problems over distribution channels, advertising etc.; and

- organizational attitudes do not have a chance to harden around products.

Changing these once the product has become established in a number of markets will be a laborious and expensive process. In its challenge for the European detergents market, the Japanese Kao may need vast resources to outgun established players such as P&G and Unilever, but at least it has the advantage of starting from scratch.

Reorganizing for Change

The accelerating rate of change in the marketplace has prompted a number of firms to rely more and more on task forces or on ad hoc committees pulled together for a limited period and cutting across the established organizational boundaries. In Europe, **Heinz** has made extensive use of this method, to examine issues concerned with strategy, or merely housekeeping issues like the international transfer of executives. "We've really changed the way we operate," claims Europe vice president Paul Corddry. "Thinking is much less insular, and you see the impact elsewhere."

It is a management technique that is probably more common in Japanese companies than in some of the more rigid Western firms, and Sony, for one, places great emphasis on grass-roots cooperation across the organization to get a job done. Experience shows that the corporate tasks to be performed seldom fit neatly into the group structure, and only by crossing boundaries can effective solutions be found.

A different line of attack to the same problem is adopted by Klaus Jacobs. He introduced one more major reorganization in his group early in 1990 before selling his stake, adding a senior level product/market matrix to the structure. He is unrepentant about the number of organizational changes he has made: "In my experience, the biggest barrier to renewal is organizational stability." Jacobs believes that there should be frequent changes at the top of the organization to encourage managers to focus on the interests of the company as a whole, and to foster teamwork rather than internal competition.

But beware . . .

Keeping managers on their toes has its drawbacks. Jacobs' decision to seek a buyer for his company came after losses of $50 million, made at his company's recent US acquisition, the E J Brach confectionery company, were attributed in part to unwise management changes. Something always falls between the cracks when structural changes occur, as one consultant puts it. The UK electronic instrumentation group **Eurotherm**, for example, has prospered handsomely from the fall-out from some major US rivals. "All reorganizations are disruptive," thinks Eurotherm's chairman Jack Leonard. "They always 'rationalize' the management, and that leaves niches for us."

Chapter 5

The Future of the Country Manager

Moves to coordinate European marketing and manufacturing have cut the traditional role of country managers, and their disappearance has been forecast. But there are cogent reasons why they should remain with undiminished, if altered, powers. On the evidence provided by the companies in this survey, country managers' job specifications may be changing radically, but for every company that is reducing the country manager's authority, there is another that is increasing it. Among the latter is IBM, whose European director of organization, Agnès Roux-Kiener, points out simply that "geography *is* the market."

If Europe does coalesce into a single market in fact as well as theory, it might be possible to rationalize the structure so that individual countries became in effect sales areas reporting to a European head office, along with service, manufacturing and distribution functions. Small hi-tech companies commonly adopt such a structure already, avoiding unnecessary overheads and bureaucratic layers of control.

In cases where there is little direct competition and a small number of customers with predictable and similar problems that demand highly specialized selling requiring relatively infrequent visits, the absence of a country organization and backup can be only a minor disadvantage. Further, the rapid improvement in data communication simplifies the marketing by allowing designs, specifications etc. to be transmitted back and forth between the central designers and estimators and the customers.

Country Operations—the Bare Minimum

Administrative problems in marketing to a foreign country begin as soon as the company needs significant numbers of people to sell, distribute or service its products there. Reliance on an independent distributor is sometimes the answer, but usually only a partial and short-term one. Joint ventures, too, have their uses, but for forceful marketing and sales, a subsidiary company, set up from scratch or acquired, is the only effective vehicle. The basic strategic considerations are as follows:

- Customers making important purchases need to feel the supplier's long-term commitment to their interests, and therefore its local presence can be essential.

- The supplier's product range may need to be supplemented or adapted with software etc. to suit local needs.

Organizing for Marketing Advantage
Business International

- Local manufacture may be necessary, either for the output or to emphasize "good citizenship."

- If government contracts are in prospect, a local presence and tax base are politically advisable, whatever the EC regulations may state.

- Good local business opportunities may exist outside the group's product range; acquisition of, or a joint venture with, a local company may also be desirable.

- Nationalistic purchasers prefer to buy from local companies not obviously controlled by outside interests.

As the product range and the number of customers increase, an expanding local presence is almost inevitable. Cash flow becomes an issue and extensive local finance facilities will be necessary, while closer attention has to be paid to the peculiarities of the market.

Employing staff immediately imposes legal, fiscal and insurance obligations on the employer, obligations that will vary from country to country for many years to come. "As long as there are nations, we will continue to have an ICI office in each country," says Tony Beck, ICI regional executive in charge of the affairs of some 15 European subsidiaries. Legal responsibilities on employers vary significantly from one country to another, particularly between the Code Napoléon countries and the others. ICI has calculated that for an operation of its size and extent, a minimum of 10 people is required in a given country to handle its affairs effectively. Apart from the standard administrative functions, government and local community relations, as well as environmental issues are becoming more important and more demanding.

The Country Manager's Persona

If local operations are so necessary, why are country managers considered by some to be under threat? For most companies, the reasons are historical. Their operations in a country have been built up typically over decades, starting with sales and marketing, but with warehousing, manufacturing, R&D and other functions being built up gradually, often with the aid of local loan finance and other banking facilities. A quotation on the stock exchange becomes a necessity for a few companies, but desirable for a good many more: one small UK lighting firm regards its quotations on continental exchanges as advertising its resolve to become dominant in the European lighting markets.

The country manager has usually had overall responsibility for all of these matters—and in some countries is even liable to be put in jail if detailed regulations on employment or safety are not complied with. He has therefore had to be a generalist and accustomed to making many broad decisions independently. In most companies, the policy has been to employ nationals in the role, but without offering any realistic opportunity to enter the top, central echelons of the company's management. Many country managers, in any case, would not be prepared to live in a foreign country at the point in their careers when they are wanting to put down permanent roots.

The job has therefore suited a particular type of individual—able and effective, but only modestly ambitious and enjoying the status of a big fish in a small pool. That is one reason why it has been a common experience in companies to find their country managers protecting their pools so carefully. If the company generates local profitable business as well as acting as middleman for group sales, the country manager is in a stronger position still.

Many companies in this survey, including Glaxo and Nestlé, have prospered mightily through leaving their country managers to develop their businesses with as much freedom as possible, making it a point of principle not to interfere. The problems that Black & Decker faced, however, were typical of many other companies questioned:

- The country managers would often compete against each other more vigorously than against outside competitors, particularly for sales to third countries, but also for internal investment funds.

- The larger countries boasted their own design and manufacturing facilities, but none was big enough to compete effectively with the Japanese.

- With a career usually spent almost exclusively in their home countries, the country managers lacked the experience and sometimes even the aptitude to take the wider strategic view of the company's business that is necessary to compete on a global scale.

European Production—the First Step

Some rationalization of production across Europe has generally been seen as the first, relatively straightforward step in integrating European operations. For autos, computers, pharmaceuticals, chemicals etc., this has usually been done from the outset, but in household appliances, photographic products and other fast-moving consumer goods, only in the past decade have the benefits of automation grown large enough and certain enough to justify the investment and overcome the country managers' resistance.

Even so, consultants warn, the benefits may not be easily attained for the following reasons:

- Rationalized production implies rationalized products, which the customer may not easily accept.

- Producing too many variants from a single plant for local markets quickly reduces the economic benefits.

- Central or regional control of production makes the company less flexible and less sensitive to customers' needs and preferences.

- The scope is limited for development projects aimed at local market niches.

- Rationalized production is heavily dependent on efficient distribution; that, according to Moulinex, is "the biggest factor."

- Rationalized production results in a serious reduction in the country manager's role and job satisfaction. If the center plans to coordinate the marketing of individual products, the country manager may well feel his job is being shot from under him.

In companies like NCR and Kodak, the country managers' autonomy was always carefully defined, long before global marketing was an issue. Product policy and pricing were dictated from the functionally organized US headquarters. The country managers' responsibilities covered what was left. But that included manufacturing and some R&D, and the country managers were powerful enough to resist any radical moves to coordinate their operations laterally.

Coordinating the Marketing

All of the companies in the survey are convinced of the need to coordinate their marketing across Europe, although the rationale is usually rather more complex than for manufacturing. There is general agreement that the strength of the product in a given market and the long-term profit potential can be assured and developed only if the product is also strong in neighboring geographical markets. The difficult issue is not so much the principle of coordination, but the degree of coordination and the methods by which it is achieved.

The country manager is therefore faced with the need for his marketing teams to coordinate their activities with their opposite numbers elsewhere in Europe, often without producing a corresponding financial return to the subsidiary. A number of companies have found that unless some robust organizational changes are made, they risk receiving mere lip-service from country managers in terms of regional marketing coordination. But if the changes affect the country manager's bottom line, they probably affect his bonus as well.

According to Gerry Alcock of London-based consultants Brand Positioning Services, "The big divide is whether the profit is centralized or local. If the local management is in charge of the profit, it will always win in any conflict." In some companies, he has found that more energy and market research programs are directed at winning the political battles over coordination than in fighting the competitor. Bartlett and Ghoshal (see Chapter 1) have come to the same conclusion: "Independent units have feigned compliance while fiercely protecting their independence. The dependent units have found that the new cooperative spirit implies little more than the right to agree with those on whom they depend."

☞ **Thorn EMI's central profit control**

To resolve this conflict of interest, the lighting division (the proposed sale of which to the US group GTE was subsequently canceled) of the UK-based Thorn EMI was one of the few respondents in the survey that had decided to take profit responsibility away from the country manager. Although the division was UK-centered, lighting had become increasingly international. Before the decision to sell out was made, Thorn EMI management had concluded that to safeguard its strong position in the UK commercial lighting market and to grow further internationally, the division would have to be strengthened by acquisition. Therefore, as a first step, it set up an international division to export its existing ranges of light fittings, to develop new products and to search for possible purchases. Having added

Holophane in France to its French interests, it put the French country manager in charge of southern Europe and the Swedish manager in charge of Scandinavia. A chief executive for Europe was appointed, and together with the director of manufacturing he started to plan production on a European scale. Four product divisions were set up, with pan-European profit responsibility. It was decided that sales had to be managed locally, and that country managers would be responsible for volume and margin only.

Other companies have been content to proceed more cautiously, leaving the country managers with sufficient powers to run their operations effectively, but gradually drawing them into a network of varying degrees of formality.

☞ Stressing commonality at Colgate-Palmolive

Changes made to Colgate-Palmolive (C-P)'s structure during 1989–90 have been aimed at making better use of its assets. C-P has a mix of international and local brands, and European president Brian Bergin, while anxious to safeguard the profits from the local brands, considers that "there is a heritage of too much diversity. We need to stress commonality now." A program to rationalize production is going ahead, but "it is not in our culture to be ruthless."

On the marketing side at C-P:

- The country managers were initially pulled together through regular European meetings.

- For the European brands, category managers have now been appointed and installed at the Brussels regional head office. The aim is to expand these brands' sales from around 50% of current turnover to 75%. Support staff are mostly located in national offices. All are expected to be out in the field at least once a week.

- Country managers retain profit responsibility, for the time being at least, and the four with the largest markets are now members of a European management board to ensure that they play a full role in strategic developments.

Bergin acknowledges that geographical ties "are a tough thing to beat. A lot of people see it as a win-lose situation, so we're in the process of giving the product categories an unfair advantage. The aim is a matrix of objectives that mutually support one another."

In the business-to-business sector, priorities may be different, but similar solutions are emerging, as the following case illustrates.

☞ Compaq's division of labor

Compaq Computer has built up a European organization from scratch in six years, becoming the number two in European sales of personal computers with a turnover of over $1 billion in 1989. Starting with German and UK subsidiaries, "the roll-out was done on the basis of very careful and sound business planning," says Compaq's international president Eckhard Pfeiffer. The group's success has been based in part on a policy of selling exclusively through dealers, and therefore strong national companies are required. The product range is planned and developed centrally in the US, but with strong input from Munich where the international operations are based. Although the terms of the contracts with dealers are similarly uniform, thereafter heavy reliance is placed on the country managers: they are selected for their experience with large corporations, and are expected to play their part in the management by consensus of a big international group.

"It's a combination of Asian, European and American philosophy," says one senior executive. The central marketing staff are no more than 30 strong, and not all based in Munich. Their specific roles are:

- to oversee marketing communications in order to ensure correct positioning, but not identical advertising;

- to coordinate marketing programs for major multinational accounts;

- to conduct market research and develop business strategy;

- to develop product proposals; and

- to coordinate training for sales and support staff.

However, the aim is to achieve the "best thing for the company and to leverage the ideas from each subsidiary" rather than to impose central strategies. Significantly, Compaq claims that its decentralized structure has allowed it to be more responsive to market needs than its rivals (principally IBM), while still being faster in developing and launching new products.

Developing the Country Manager's Role

There are probably five main reasons why companies are concerned to preserve their country managers' position and influence in the marketing and sales spheres (irrespective of any responsibilities they may also have for R&D, procurement or manufacturing):

- Managers are often responsible for a significant share of the company's business. International brands and customers may be increasing, but few companies can afford to neglect profits that are derived only locally. In service companies, the local element may be as high as 90% of the total.

- Sales performance depends heavily on the country manager's motivation and profit responsibility: "I wouldn't accept a job where I was responsible only for volume and margins," says one senior manager in a company that has rejected that alternative. The country manager's experience, enthusiasm and judgment in building profitable business is a valuable corporate resource.

- Few companies have enough faith at present in their control and logistic systems to keep inventories down and service to the customer up without local warehousing and administration.

- In many industries, community relations are increasingly important. Environmental and social issues, government relations, PR and sponsorship all require sensitive treatment from managers experienced in the local culture.

- Global trends are leading to greater market fragmentation. Even the trend to globalization for many products will actually increase the number of niches as customers become more discriminating.

Only companies with a local entrepreneurial presence can hope to exploit such opportunities effectively. "The local touch is what makes you win or lose," says 3M's regional vice president for the European marketing subsidiaries, Edoardo Pieruzzi. "We debate a lot in our organization on the role of the country general managers. We think they will remain at the head of profit centers, but with more influence over service standards and the information flow to detect opportunities locally."

Finding and exploiting differences and individual preferences is fundamental to good marketing, and therefore to the role of the country manager. It's a skill that forms one reason for the Japanese multinationals' success in Europe, according to Professor Doyle's research (see Chapter 4). If globalization is allowed to imply as little discrimination between segments as the study suggests, it becomes a top-down, production-led process at odds with the marketer's instincts. In that form, it could be a short-lived phenomenon. But a growing proportion of the coordination work described by the companies in this survey involves taking local successful ideas and "best practice" and exploiting them elsewhere. That assumes that there is a coherent local management capable of contributing to the bottom-up-top-down decision-making process.

☞ Adding value locally at Rank Xerox

Rank Xerox is one company that freely admits to having learned some hard lessons in the head office/country manager relationship. "In the past," says European marketing director Lyndon Haddon, "we sent a huge team into a country to develop a strategy to improve profit. People would spend all their time arguing over it, and every time we've tried to do a common system here it's been a disaster. So now we say, 'In the end, it's up to you.'" At the center, "our job is to make a generic product," explains Haddon, and it is then for the country managers to "add value locally." Some general managers source their support products such as software locally.

The marketing and support strategies are tailored to suit each particular market. In the German insurance sector, for example, the big companies usually sell their policies through dedicated, sole agents, and the Rank Xerox subsidiary has developed systems specifically for them. But in the UK and the US, agents usually sell more than one product (at least for nonlife business), so the systems needed are different. Haddon's role is to develop the segmentation process and coordinate best practices across Europe—and increasingly, with the US and Far East.

Roche, still in the process of reevaluating its structure, considers local flexibility to be all-important. The object of any new organization, it says, will be to promote entrepreneurial thinking down the line and to give the man in the field the most efficient support to back entrepreneurial action. Managers must have the resources to respond rapidly to changing customer demands and tougher competition. Even **Lego**, with its policy of retaining at the center everything that does not need to be in the national subsidiaries, recognizes the danger of a demotivated local management, and in practice benefits from the local development of products and ideas.

☞ Focusing responsibility at NCR

NCR managed to achieve its now-dominant position in the world market for automatic teller machines (ATMs) by devolving authority to its subsidiary in Scotland. In 1980, NCR's old Dundee factory in Scotland was on the point of closure, a victim of the electronic revolution. Its remaining product line, an early small ATM, depended on the parent plant in the US for most of its technology, and according to Jim Adamson, vice president and managing director of self-service systems, NCR's small share of the market at that time could be attributed to the rather slow and cumbersome committee in the financial services division that then ran the ATM operation. "It was too far removed from the market," says Adamson.

NCR decided to give Adamson and the Scottish plant a lifeline in the form of a remit to take over the design, development and international marketing of ATMs. Adamson and a small team in Dundee were at last able to provide the focus on the product and its marketing that it did not receive as an appendage of the computer business. Adamson has a centralized, product management organization, but generally works through the NCR national marketing companies: "There's no way I could run a selling operation in 88 countries."

However, there's no obligation on them to supply his ATMs or him to use NCR computers for self-service systems. "Fred Newall [senior vice president for NCR Europe] can always tell me to get lost—it's made the development organization very customer oriented." In fact, in some countries, the ATMs are handled by distributors rather than the national NCR company, and one such, Finland's Nokia, has recently taken its first orders for ATMs in the Soviet Union.

Adamson's team markets direct to potential customers, but as a matter of policy, the national company's account managers are also closely involved. Comments Newall evenly, "It works quite well because our objectives are the same." The enthusiastic Adamson now claims one third of the world's installed base and nearly two thirds of new installations, and has taken over responsibility for the US market.

Getting close to the customer

In the service industries, the role of the country manager has never been in any real doubt because of the vital need to be near the customer and to respond to day-to-day needs. For example, all of the major advertising groups aim to provide a full range of services in each European capital, in addition to services in the provincial business centers. The network can then serve multinational clients as well as pulling in local business. In consultant Tim Breene's agency, part of Aegis, local business accounts for around 75% of the total; for the multinational clients, the home agency becomes the network leader for the account, and "around eight" high-calibre executives are located around the network, reporting both to the country manager and to the center.

☞ **Emphasizing the national at Chep Europe**

A similar reliance on the country managers to build local business is evident at Chep Europe, part of a joint venture between GKN, the UK engineering group, and the Australian Brambles Enterprises. Chep operates a pallet hire service in a number of European countries, mainly for the food industry supplying the retailers. The business is unevenly developed in that it is well established in the UK and France but only just starting in Germany and Italy. Chep Europe's chief executive Nick Butcher recalls that he did consider setting up one European organization, only to reject the idea because, being a service industry, Chep has to make its decisions as close to the customer as possible. In addition, argues Butcher, "the markets will be predominantly national as far ahead as we can see."

Cross-frontier business comes in two forms for Chep: local suppliers of wines and food produce reaching out across mainland Europe, and MNCs developing European manufacture and supply. The latter is still small in extent, and an international marketing and development director is sufficient to represent Chep at the international level on tne few occasions when it is necessary. Even then, he works through the profit-responsible country manager. "I like to try to avoid 'coordination,'" says Butcher. "Our intention is to standardize as much as possible—from computer systems to personnel policies."

Progress Through the Lead Country System

One way of compensating country managers for any job erosion through increased coordination is to install a lead country system, which extends individual responsibilities onto the wider European stage. Many of the companies in the survey regularly nominate certain subsidiaries to be or become expert in a specific product, application, or marketing or sales tactic. It's an old idea which satisfies a number of objectives:

- It helps even out the development of multinational business, discussed earlier; the subsidiaries with long and successful experience with a product or application will be in a good position to pass on their expertise for use in unexploited markets.

- It motivates local staff as well as the country managers by involving them more closely in the wider development of the group.

- It keeps central staff at a minimum, while demonstrating the way forward for cooperation to possibly reluctant subsidiaries in a practical way.

- It keeps development costs on new products and applications in check and avoids duplication of effort.

- It ensures that customers' international needs are adequately provided for.

The system arises naturally in the business-to-business area where the same products are often sold for different applications in different industries. As an executive at TI's John Crane division (making seals for machinery) has found, "As night follows day, one of the companies will have more pump manufacturers on its patch, say, and will become the lead country for that application. Engineers love to design a new product, but the key to making money in this business is to stop them duplicating designs."

Computer companies also face similar problems in developing applications and software to suit particular industries and market segments. The German subsidiary might therefore be given responsibility for, say, the chemical industry, Scandinavia for paper, France for the food industry, the UK for finance. IBM, whose organization in Europe is described more fully in the following chapter, in July 1990 announced the adoption of a similar formula: the German country manager heads European marketing for mainframes and industrial customers; the Italian for the middle-range computers, and the government and scientific applications; the UK for PCs and AIX software systems; and the French for communications systems.

Executives who become expert in their field can then be seconded to other countries to build the business there. There are, of course, attendant difficulties, as Alan Stark, managing director of **American Express** in the UK points out. His subsidiary is in the process of being reintegrated into the Europe, Middle East and Africa division after a period outside it. Stark's executives are particularly experienced in database marketing, where computers are used to refine lists of potential clients.

"My people are playing a role across Europe, either on a time-limited or a periodic basis. I'm concerned about my payroll, so if it becomes a working practice, I charge a fee. The danger is if staff get stolen or get distracted by the joys of travel." In other companies, it has been found that the lead country is not always strong enough and possessed of a broad enough vision to carry the extra responsibilities.

Confused responsibilities can also be a problem. Doyle's research into the behavior of UK, US and Japanese subsidiaries (see Chapter 4) found one US company operating in Europe where the French were responsible for market segmentation, the British for promotional planning and the Germans for product development: "None of the Japanese employed this type of international structure, all giving their UK subsidiaries clear responsibility." This mirrored the traditional organization in Japan where "every business is a profit center." Doyle found that the problem with the US approach was that no one felt they had clear responsibility for and control of performance in the UK market. "Headquarters or the regional office was often blamed by local managers for imposing the wrong strategy or for inadequate information—e.g. 'The French are given responsibility for segmentation and they never tell us.'"

A more radical development of the lead country idea is to give the marketing management of the lead country specific Europewide responsibility, a method Procter & Gamble has long favored.

☞ Procter & Gamble's lead country approach

Procter & Gamble (P&G) first nominated a lead country as long ago as 1973 when launching its Pampers brand of disposable diaper across Europe. The product was developed and launched in Germany, and the senior manager in charge moved on to the European HQ in Brussels to supervise the roll-out. The system did not work well because of the friction generated between the Pampers team and the country management, faced with different priorities. For later launches, the system was developed into "Eurobrand teams," headed by the lead country general manager and consisting of representatives from the main subsidiaries and from manufacturing etc.

The aim was to exploit local expertise and responsiveness: in fact, the reverse seems to have been the case. Because of all of the parties involved, decision making was pushed up the tree to country manager level, and profitability was easily lost to sight. In consequence, "category" managers have now been introduced in each country, with profit responsibility over the three main product groups—laundry, personal care and paper products. These category managers report to both the country general manager and the geographical divisional managers in a classic matrix structure.

The traditional P&G brand management system has been downgraded, and the internecine warfare between brands will, observers hope, be replaced by a more mature approach to market segmentation and the optimization of profits from a product category. Meanwhile, the category managers are relieving the country managers of much of their detailed responsibilities, allowing them to spend more time on functions like external relations.

Concentrating the expertise

In one form or another, the lead country system is likely to continue to flourish. The obvious benefits in concentrating expertise in particular offices, and in assigning to one or other of them pioneering roles for the benefit of the group are too strong to be abandoned. Even Nestlé, according to a Harvard case study, uses subsidiaries to provide "prime mover markets" to help the central product director convince country managers to launch a newly developed product. The study appears to favor more centralization: Nestlé remains resolutely decentralized, however, and profitable. The days of the country manager are far from numbered.

Chapter 6

Coordinators and the Product Manager

For many companies, the only practical way to combine central and local authority in such a diverse market as Europe is some form of matrix organization, loathed by many, but regarded as logically unavoidable by some. In consumer goods industries, country subsidiaries almost inevitably duplicate each other's efforts in the great battle to please the customer and beat off the competition. There is also the worry that competitors may be creeping up in other markets unobserved, exploiting opportunities more quickly and effectively, that precious ideas and resources are being wasted on conflicting product positioning, systems development, advertising and promotion etc. But how can the use of these assets be improved without restricting the country manager's freedom of maneuver and dampening his entrepreneurial enthusiasm?

The International Coordinator

The starting point for companies with a country-based marketing structure that want a more coherent European attack is for central management to appoint coordinators. The coordinator is often a senior executive with valuable experience who has perhaps outgrown a country manager's job, but for whom there is not yet a corporate role. Generally, the coordinator's often ill-defined task is to advise country subsidiaries and ensure that best practice is adopted throughout their region. The strongly centralized Italian oil company Agip has a coordinating system, with a special staff department at corporate level to coordinate marketing among its foreign subsidiaries.

Coordination also seems to suit Scandinavian companies. **Lego**'s coordinating structure is relatively straightforward, with a small liaison group helping to smooth the paths between the central European company and the 14 sales companies. **Electrolux** is naturally a great deal more complicated, even within its white goods "product line," partly on account of the only half-absorbed acquisitions such as Zanussi. At Electrolux, country managers are responsible for most manufacturing and marketing subsidiaries in their territories, but central product area managers coordinate product development and manufacturing. The "Marketing Europe" team, formed in 1987, pulls together the many strands (and brands) making up Electrolux's marketing platform. In spite of some moves to further strengthen central control, the Electrolux management insists on leaving real authority in each national market.

Some companies have managed to achieve the desired coordination without adding staff or structures. As consultant John Hegarty points out, referring mainly to consumer industries, if a brand concept has been clearly defined and articulated—and understood and accepted by local managements—central management can afford to be pragmatic about the details of its implementation. Thus the need for sometimes costly coordination is reduced. **Scott Paper,**

Heinz and **Reckitt & Colman** all prefer to bring their executives together rather than rely on central staff to coordinate their European strategy. These companies have corporate cultures that are conducive to cooperation—a local Scott MD who was not prepared to cooperate was replaced. This approach serves to underline the importance of recognizing that structures are only as good as the people they serve; personalities count for more than charts.

The problem of ambiguity

But other companies find that the ambiguities of the Electrolux system, and indeed of coordination methods generally, can defeat their purposes. Most important, the issues raised by effective coordination are often too weighty to be hung from a merely advisory link. Changing the priorities between products, for example, could have a marked effect on a subsidiary's bottom line in a way that could be justified only in the wider group context. As long as the country manager remains profit accountable—implying a remit from the center that he should give priority to profit maximization within his territory—the unfortunate coordinator is unlikely to get very far. He will therefore be reduced to details that have little effect on the progress of the group—even if he is a good enough diplomat not to arouse local antipathies.

This was **Kodak**'s experience. Kodak began experimenting with a coordinating function in the early 1970s, when a European regional organization was first set up. Then, the national subsidiaries were closely regulated by the US headquarters but in other respects were largely self-sufficient. Intensifying competition in the photographic market, with the battle front switching to processing rather than to film sales, meant that the lumbering giant badly needed both a convincing global strategy and sharp local tactics. For a time, it had neither, and the need raised organizational issues far greater than could be solved by coordination, however effective.

The difficulties involved in the lead country system and the ineffectiveness of coordinators have prompted many companies, especially in the consumer goods sector, to set up European product managers, giving them varying degrees of authority. Ironically, the industrial marketing companies have at the same time been moving to modify and adapt their normally product-based organizations in order to get closer to the market.

Product Managers and Business Marketing

Business marketing usually implies relatively small, specialist groups of customers, and particular customs and techniques to meet their needs. Companies structure their operations to suit. The UK engineering group **GKN**, for example, found in the late 1970s that desperately needed changes to the old-established group were obstructed by its then predominantly regional structure, which supported a large and interventionist head office. In the auto industry of the 1950s and 1960s, such an organization might have made sense, but the growing globalization of car manufacture, essentially concentrated in Japan, the US and Continental Europe, demanded that GKN should restructure if its world lead in constant-velocity joints for front-wheel drive vehicles was to be maintained. The transmission management had to be allowed to focus on, and invest in, that business undistracted by the severe problems elsewhere in the group. Now, it is centered in Germany (where GKN had made a

---

☞ IBM—EVOLVING TOWARD TEAMWORK

IBM is in "a profound evolutionary phase," according to Elio Catania, IBM's European vice president for market development. Technological and marketplace moves toward more open systems (so that companies need not tie themselves to a particular manufacturer) and to networks of personal computers (away from the central mainframe) forced IBM to rethink how it could get closer to its dealers and their customers. The traditionally powerful and independently minded product groups have been slimmed down, the typewriter and printer businesses will be spun off completely, and the geographical companies are firmly on top. But "we want to keep the vertical product view to ensure the best technology," says Catania. The country manager has the prime responsibility for profits, and divides his territory by region and by market segment. Segment managers are then given budget responsibility, and can pull in experts as required—"You have to create the general manager attitude at a lower level."

The power of the center has been cut back profoundly as the balance has shifted toward country managers buying in central services. As a result, the Paris headquarters has been cut by 20% in the past two years and will be slimmed further. Country managers—the Big Four of whom now have specific Europewide responsibilities (see Chapter 5)—also sit on a pan-European board, "sharing decisions on a common basis." Teamwork is now the style, having replaced "conflict management" between product divisions and country managers. In the past, IBM's reliance on the matrix model resulted in an acceptance of inevitable conflicts between the two axes. Supposedly "clear lines of accountability" were anything but, and measurement systems have now been altered to encourage integration rather than internal competition, and give accountability only to the customer team.

---

major acquisition), and the group's small UK head office maintains an essentially financial control over its affairs.

The vital need was to maximize returns on the heavy investment required in development and manufacturing the CV joints, and to match the handful of worldwide auto manufacturers. For the group's **Chep** pallet hire operation (see Chapter 5), on the other hand, a high degree of local autonomy was necessary to satisfy a wide range of local producers and retailers.

Even in a mass market business like copiers, certain equipment may need specialist attention in a small product division, without which it would be in danger of being pushed to one side. Costs and profit need to be shown separately, and appropriate marketing and sales techniques developed. **Rank Xerox** relies on its geographical units to market its main copier ranges, but its work stations are much more specialized in terms of application, and are likely to be bought by relatively few, multinational clients. Therefore, a central product-line structure handles the work stations throughout Europe, calling on the services of the national subsidiaries when needed.

Product divisions whether of the macro or micro kind may reassure the central management that the return on investment in the product will be maximized, but they have drawbacks that apply to consumer as well as business markets:

☐ The management of each product division can be insensitive to the shifting sands of the marketplace because the product defines its area of responsibility.

Organizing for Marketing Advantage
Business International

☐ It may be difficult to obtain an objective view of the whole company's performance in the market outside the product division's immediate segment, or to formulate a strategy for it, if no one is responsible.

☐ Innovation that falls outside the division's experience may be missed or allowed to wither for the same reason.

☐ When the divisions grow large, their managers can become remote from their markets, and coverage of smaller, individual markets may suffer.

☐ Success in some markets may depend on other divisions, with whom different priorities and cultures make cooperation difficult.

☐ Products from different divisions (as in IBM's old, widely criticized example) may be incompatible, and salesmen calling on the same customer may work to different standards and effectively compete with each other.

☐ Market share on a country-by-country basis may be sacrificed to product divisional profitability, which is often not analyzed according to country. Thus individual markets may be overlooked.

For some or all of these reasons, a number of companies have radically altered their product structures. Some, like **American Express**, abandoned product divisions in favor of national companies long ago. Others, in the industrial sector, have redefined a division's responsibilities round the market rather than the product, or merely attempted to loosen the straps round their product divisions. While **SKF**, therefore, supplies the needs of the after-market for bearings all over the world from a single division, **Du Pont** encourages coordination between product groups through the formation of small marketing groups, which bring together representatives from different product divisions to focus on the needs of particular industries—forcing executives to talk to each other as well as to the customers. The trend is visble in other MNCs:

☞ **ICI Europa's coordinating role**

ICI's Europa operation was set up originally to focus the attentions of ICI's massive product divisions on continental European markets where, for largely historical reasons, ICI was relatively weak. By concentrating on a few products in particular markets, the Europa team, from its German and Belgian offices, could develop some businesses itself, but more important, act as a go-between and stimulus. Now that ICI's divisions have been split up into nine smaller but more international "businesses," they have the choice of relying on the national sales and marketing companies under Europa's control, or setting up their own companies. Thus the pharmaceutical business has its own network, but agro-chemicals has, with some exceptions, a department of its own in the national companies.

Regional executive Tony Beck explains, "We are a very useful goad on the businesses, but we also work with them to help them cut their cost base and make their marketing more effective." Some observers feel that, even so, the big European markets do not figure strongly enough in the thinking of the businesses, and a European advisory board, which pointedly excludes the UK, has recently been set up by Tom Hutchison, the main board director responsible for Europe. It remains to be seen whether the European structure is developed further and given a holding board like ICI's operations in the Americas and in the Far East.

☞ **Devolving power at Hoechst**

In a similar attempt to grapple with its centralized culture and make its 15 product divisions more responsive to the market, Hoechst has embarked upon its most extensive reorganization in 20 years. It has decided to split the product divisions into 100 business units, about one third of them centered outside Germany. The divisional sales and marketing staff will be dispersed to the business units, which will be profit centers enjoying a high degree of autonomy. The business unit manager will be free to organize it in his own way, and even, apparently, to specify its relationship with the center.

Product Managers and Consumer Goods

In consumer marketing, central product managers are gaining popularity as a way of putting additional strength behind coordinated marketing strategies. For different reasons, Moulinex and Bang & Olufsen both deploy international product marketing managers, whose authority vis-a-vis the country managers is gradually being increased. Moulinex aims to move its range up-market, and its image accordingly; Bang & Olufsen, the Danish hi-fi manufacturer, needs to guard its worldwide image for sophisticated design and quality very carefully—particularly after its link with the electronics giant Philips.

Few companies are going as far as the highly centralized **Gillette**, or even **Thorn EMI Lighting** (see Chapter 5), which decided to give full profit responsibility to its central managers. Instead, the product managers tend either to share the profit role, or be assigned a more vague remit covering product strategy and development, production control, pricing etc. Many companies are notably cautious in their handling of the product management issue because of the wide-ranging implications for the status of the country manager. The two exist in constant tension, and the current balance between them is often regarded as a staging point in the move to a more integrated structure, where any increase in the product manager's power has to be matched by a corresponding widening of the country manager's role.

Progress may therefore depend on the speed at which the managers on either axis can be trained or persuaded (or, failing everything, replaced) to accept the new delineation of their roles and adopt the necessary strategic view of the business. Brian Bergin at Colgate-Palmolive warns that "it requires first-class people to think through the complex, matrix-type decision processes." If the company is fortunate enough to have plenty of such people, they need to be moved into positions where they can be most effective. According to Klaus Jacobs, chief executive of **Jacobs Suchard** before he decided to sell control to Philip Morris:

> We resolved to concentrate our best management talent in the firing line, making those people responsible for the country-based business units and then ruthlessly stripping away as many as possible of the intervening management layers between them and top management in Zurich. We were determined to encourage business unit heads in this way to think more entrepreneurially about their

ADVERTISING—THE ACID TEST

Whatever the theory behind a company's European structure, clues to the real balance of power between the center and its outposts often have to be sought elsewhere, and advertising policy provides one revealing test. The freedom allowed over the selection of a local advertising agency, and the brief given to the agency as to the advertising expected from it, do not always correspond to the company's professed organizational policy.

Heineken beer and Volvo auto advertising demonstrate a sharp contrast between local campaigns and centrally sourced ads, reflecting differences in distribution rights and management strategies. The evidence from this report suggests that, at least in the consumer goods industries, the advertising process is being made to conform more closely to the corporate structure and systems.

This is not to imply that international campaigns, or even themes for campaigns, are on the increase. Rather, as MNCs' European structures evolve toward a balance between central and local forces, so the advertising agencies serving them must:

- Be ready to adapt their own methods of working, and assist with the liaison and coordination process as and when required.

- Provide a channel for international marketing spending—on market research, advertising production, and the small but growing international TV and press media.

- Act as guardians of the "values" that a brand stands for, to ensure that they are not devalued as they are interpreted and applied in different markets. One Spanish agency, for example, when called upon to produce a local version of the famous Johnny Walker image, turned him into a kind of ghost—far removed from the warm and friendly image that proprietors United Distillers wished to convey.

- Provide ideas suitable for multinational application when required. This can be achieved by maintaining an international outlook, if not a network of offices.

It has long been a matter for debate in the advertising world as to whether companies are better advised to look for the best agency available in each market they are addressing and then aim to coordinate the results, or to put their faith in an international chain, calculating that uniformity will make up for the lack of individual flair and that the agency will carry the overheads associated with coordination. In practice, most companies use a combination of international and local agencies to cover their European markets, partly out of necessity (client conflict etc.) and partly, perhaps, the need for quality and diversity. Coca-Cola's well-known monogamous association with the US agency McCann Erickson (which expanded across Europe originally to serve its US clients' international aspirations) is unusual.

The single agency policy may be tidy, but it can bring problems in its wake, and these have deterred **Levi Strauss** from pursuing a similar strategy to Coca-Cola. Apart from Coke, it would be difficult to find a more universally American image than that of jeans. But whereas the US agency Foote Cone & Belding (FCB) handles its advertising in the US, the London-based agency Bartle, Bogle Hegarty (BBH) produces the TV commercials for use throughout Europe through a string of local agencies. Although it has no network of its own outside the UK, BBH says, "We invest a lot of time in researching the market and talking to the Levi Strauss subsidiaries and retailers."

⇨

Colgate-Palmolive (C-P) is representative of the companies that use their agencies as an integral part of their marketing resources. "They are partners in the total process," says European president Brian Bergin. "Their first role is to support local initiatives." But the agencies concerned, FCB and Young & Rubicam, also have the brief to align C-P's advertising with global assignments, and "we meet regularly as a group on European issues. The agency is a good outreach and input for things we might overlook. With our tradition of employment from within, it's important we don't fall into the trap of navel examination."

But Bergin is adamant that "we wouldn't use an agency as an intelligence source," referring to the criticism that some US companies rely on their US agencies to act at best as marketing auditor and at worst as an internal CIA, to check that their national subsidiaries follow instructions. "Multinationals shouldn't use their agencies as Trojan horses for greater standardization," advise Harvard academics John Quelch and Edward Hoff. "An undercover operation is likely to jeopardize agency-client relations at the country level."

At the opposite extreme from the single or dual agency policy stands **Nestlé,** which at one time was alleged to use no less than 137 agencies to advertise its products in Europe, itself a reaction to the practice in the 1960s when a central, 60-strong department vetted all subsidiaries' advertising. Now, the center merely provides advice and guidance, concentrating on the "strategic" brands like Nescafé and Chambourcy.

Faced with a similar, if not quite so extensive range of agencies, **3M** recently decided to concentrate its international business through three agencies with European networks rather than the 40 it once employed. It chose the US Grey, the Brussels-based HDM and the UK BSB Dorland, which are expected to work with the European management action teams (Emats—see Chapter 7) in developing advertising plans for a product. HDM, for example, will produce in Brussels a commercial for Post-it Notes in response to the brief from the Emat concerned, on which the UK subsidiary is represented as the lead country. HDM will then pass the commercial on to its London agency, Horner Collis & Kirvan, to be adapted for the UK market.

Advertising is a much less significant part of the policy mix in industrial and business-to-business marketing, but even there, differences are indicative of wider policies. **Digital Equipment,** for example, aims at a global market place and maintains central control over its advertising in all countries, not just Europe, explaining that "when it was left to the countries, it was a mess and we lost synergy, so now we're back to a worldwide image and advertising." It does, however, place great emphasis at a national level on sponsoring arts and other events.

Canon, by contrast, allows its national subsidiaries a very free hand in their advertising, relying on an agreed common marketing strategy to ensure coherence. Local interpretation is coordinated only through regular marketing committee meetings. It does, however, sponsor international sports events such as football and motor racing, which naturally require more careful coordination. In the past, **Rank Xerox** attempted to apply a central advertising strategy and even provide centrally sourced advertising material. But now, the European headquarters merely asks its national subsidiaries to project a strong, common image and message. Execution is a local responsibility, and although "people do use each other's ads and promotions, there is no intention to make it mandatory." Coordination is secured through a European advertising council.

businesses, and do away with the filtering layers that so often seem to discourage or screen out entrepreneurial ideas (McKinsey Quarterly, winter 1987)."

It could be argued that product managers (or "global product presidents," as Jacobs prefers) represent just such a filtering or coordinating layer. In Jacobs Suchard, they replaced or strengthened a lead brand management system. In early 1990, just before the sale was announced, five regional presidents were added (America, Asia/Pacific, Brussels, Bremen in north Germany, and Paris). Jacobs recognized the contradiction, and located the presidents and other top managers in the centers where the volume of business justified it to ensure that they kept in close touch with their markets. But the effect is largely symbolic: there is no essential difference if the orders come from Zurich or from Brussels. It remains to be seen whether and how Philip Morris attempts to amalgamate Suchard with its own coffee interests such as Maxwell House, Hag and Kenco.

In the airline industry, there is a similar urgency in building a strong international marketing presence ready for the time when the European industry is effectively deregulated. International airlines remain in a peculiar marketing position; they are in effect supplying two products—domestic and outgoing flights, and incoming flights. In these two product ranges, customers, motivations, images etc. can be quite different. It might be expected that this will eventually be reflected in the airlines' structures. As consultant Gerry Alcock points out, "airlines have got to be much more tactically based" in their marketing programs.

The Italian state airline **Alitalia** has responded by abandoning its old functional organization in favor of what are, in effect, product divisions. There are two operational divisions, for passengers and cargo, and two "complementary" ones, marketing services (including catering and ground services) and leisure. Two route managers are responsible for planning and operating the European passenger services, as well as for marketing them, and the country managers report to them. Alitalia expects the new structure to increase its marketing strength, without going to the extremes of Jan Carlsen at Scandinavian Airline System, who has widely publicized his theory of the "flattened pyramid"—aimed at giving the staff the authority to act on their own initiative in the cause of good customer service.

Toward the matrix

Combining international product managers with country managers inevitably leads to a matrix structure in which responsibility is split between the regional head and the product head. This is the subject of the following chapter.

Chapter 7

The Matrix and Beyond

The nature of business involves balancing many incompatible objectives, like maximizing short- and long-term returns, or cutting costs but increasing quality. The European dimension adds a further set, forcing companies to respond to many different local requirements and preferences, while developing new products and services, and cutting costs and overheads through greater volume. That is what makes a matrix inevitable, in the view of some experts, whether the company acknowledges the fact or not, and that is why at least a third of the companies in this survey rely on some kind of matrix structure. As long as one or other axis has dominance, the conflicts and uncertainties may be slight—but the benefits likewise. Hence Colgate-Palmolive, for one example, is having to "tilt the matrix" to ensure that the geographic axis does not have things all its own way.

The Matrix: Magnificent or Mistaken?

There is, of course, a variety of kinds of matrix. Functional heads could be on one axis and geographical heads on the other. Lower down the corporate pyramid, the product/market segment matrix is sometimes found (often in the computer industry). But they all have one purpose, which is to rationalize in organizational terms the inherent conflicts between the two axes, or views of the company's interests.

- **The country manager** aims simply to maximize the profit from his particular territory. He will therefore wish to put most resources behind the opportunities and the products that will achieve that end, some of which may not even be manufactured by the group.

- **The product manager,** wishing to maximize the global profit for the product group, focuses on what he sees as the best strategic opportunities and new developments. But across the board, the aim is to reduce unit costs by cutting local variants and raising volumes, which may entail heavier local expenditure on sales and promotion than the country manager is willing or able to afford.

There are, of course, a hundred other potential sources of conflict, all of which lead consultants and others to be very wary of matrix organizations. It is open to debate whether the complexities the matrix introduces, and the management time devoted to resolving the inevitable conflicts and tensions that occur, are rewarded by a better allocation of resources and better corporate performance. One Electrolux executive likened the matrix to "leprosy," although the Swedish group probably has more matrices in its organization than most—some, indeed, are three dimensional. One drawback of the matrix approach to organizational problems was highlighted by Electrolux's white goods head Leif Johansson: "There is too much of a tendency to try to solve organizational problems by designing a structure that *quietens* conflicts rather than bringing them to the surface."*

As long as one or other axis has dominance, the conflicts and uncertainties may be slight, but the benefits will be similarly small. Hence Colgate-Palmolive, for example, has decided to "tilt the matrix" to ensure that the geographic axis does not have things all its own way, but companies that have achieved a carefully balanced matrix are few. One of them is Honeywell.

☞ Honeywell—achieving balance

Jean-Pierre Rosso, president of Honeywell Europe, believes that people who dismiss the matrix structure are "escaping reality . . . some sort of balance has to be achieved."

Until the 1970s, Honeywell operated in Europe through national subsidiaries, but with central product marketing support. The product groups became business units, now five in number, and were gradually strengthened till they shared profit responsibility with the national subsidiaries. Rosso explains, "The exact balancing point depends on the business—the higher the tech, the more important the business unit." Subsidiaries and business units report to Rosso, along with pan-European functional heads such as marketing or engineering. "The sales affiliates [subsidiaries] call the shots when it comes to selling; the business units call the shots on strategic issues, embodied in the marketing or engineering areas etc."

The country managers and the business unit heads meet in a European policy committee, where "the responsibilities are clear and dependency is a part of life," says Rosso. In practice, neither business unit nor subsidiary will be responsible for 100% of the profit. The balance is worked out case-by-case: "It can happen that optimization at the business level gives one answer, and optimization at the affiliate level gives another." Rosso has "a tie-breaking function," but insists that "it doesn't happen very often that I have to decide."

Rosso argues that the corporate emphasis on partnership overrides the negative aspects of the competition between the business units and the subsidiaries. Outside pressures can also have a constructive effect. Honeywell is involved in equipping the vast Canary Wharf office development in London's Docklands. "An affiliate even of Honeywell UK's size could not cope with a project that size alone," explains Rosso. "It required full support from Europe and Canada for expertise, forcing cooperation. You don't tolerate nonteaming attitudes in a global business, and when people understand they can't do it alone, it helps a lot." Even so, Rosso still believes in the benefits of competition: "The conflict is very positive—you need the strongest possible people in the business units and in the affiliates. We must continue to have strong affiliates—some people say they will become cost centers with only sales goals and budgets. I foresee that they will have different sorts of people, but as long as countries exist, the affiliate will continue to be strong."

---

* *Financial Times*, June 21, 1989.

The matrix culture

In IBM's experience, divisional conflict has not always been healthy, and changes are now under way to replace it with cooperation and "interlocking activity" (see Chapter 5). Some companies, say consultants, have been practically torn apart by conflicts between profit centers: a high price often has to be paid for that elusive quality, synergy. In addition to a clear structure, a favorable corporate culture and careful management are necessary to make a matrix work effectively. As Fred Newall, NCR's senior vice president, Europe, admits, "Our matrix breaks down every so often, basically because of personalities. Everyone wants to be a hero and totally responsible for success. As long as there is stability, people can work together with mutual respect. It's when there are changes that conflict occurs." Consultant Tim Breene has a solution to that problem: "I use 'shock absorbers,' that is, the informal organization which you can use to change priorities in a matrix."

Executives at Electrolux stress that its three-dimensional matrix—country, product line and functional—works only because the people involved want it to and can tolerate the ambiguities. Says Electrolux UK's managing director Jimmy James, "A lot of the way we organize depends on who you have. You fit the organization to the people. You trust in managers and give them space. If I talk to one of my MDs, we agree on the phone, and that's the end of it. We're able to make, and get, very quick decisions—we're totally unbureaucratic."

☞ Kodak relies on the human element

"Kodak has a culture that allows that [the matrix] to work," according to Bob Worden, until recently Kodak's European business research director but now on a US assignment. "People are used to working in a framework, or a team, to accomplish their ends," he adds. "They don't get overly frustrated at this type of relationship or the series of checks and balances that are imposed. We try to get people to think of themselves as European members of the Kodak family."

The company's business units set up in the mid-1980s are now meshed with the national companies (see diagram page 66). There are business unit managers in each country, for, say, consumer imaging (such as color film) or business imaging (i.e. copiers). They report functionally to the national general manager, but also through the European region business unit manager to the central product groups. The national managers report up through the region to the international group. Individual factories report to the central manufacturing group, and the research laboratories to the international research group. There is thus considerable organizational "distance" between research, manufacture, business unit, and marketing and sales. It is also noteworthy that Kodak is still organized as a US company with some international operations, an issue that the new chief executive, Kay Whitmore, may have to ponder as he faces the task of restoring the group's fortunes.

At the operating level, both country manager and business unit carry profit responsibility, and these two reporting streams are not even brought together at the European level. "In some areas it might be difficult, and it probably generates additional work," Worden concedes. "Some might say that Kodak has not yet shaken off its bureaucratic or paternal ways, and when the push comes to shove, personnel have to examine their career opportunities. A lot is laid down, but a local general manager has a high degree of responsibility

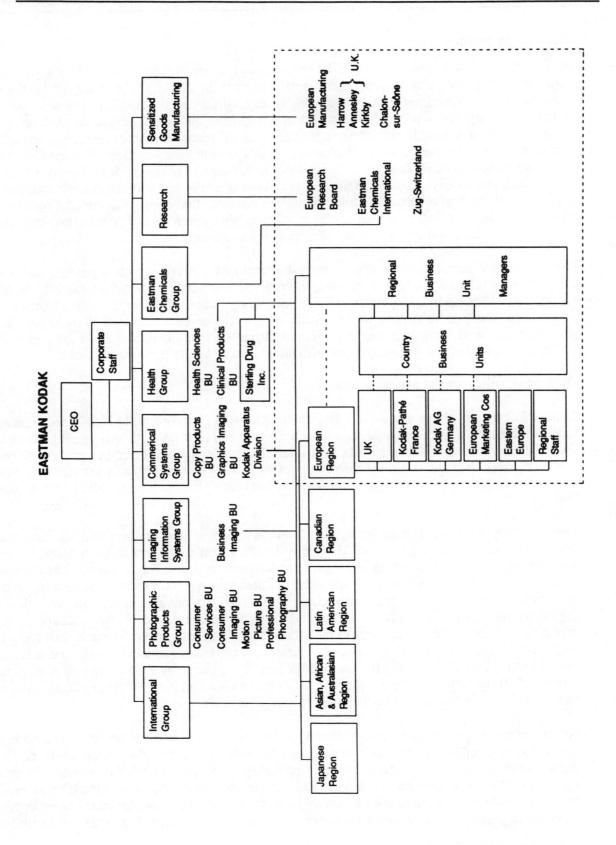

THE CENTRAL THINK TANK

Smaller companies or companies with simpler structures that are determined to avoid the complications of the matrix still need some central marketing function to act as an intelligence-gathering center, strategy think tank or even a new product development unit. In the past, such a function might have been called corporate planning, with a full range of economic forecasting, futurology, scenario planning, market and social research, and so on. In the more skeptical 1990s, most of that has been swept away, but the need to keep a corporate eye on world trends and product developments obviously remains. For some companies, the current solution is a small central marketing operation with a handful of executives, whose brief is wide ranging but of limited depth.

- At **Black & Decker,** for example, European chairman Roger Thomas brought product development into a small group marketing organization. "The best people" were selected from the major subsidiaries but allowed to stay in their national offices rather than move to the headquarters near London. "I don't believe in planning in an ivory tower," says Thomas. "You must know what the European market needs for product development. They have to keep a check on what's going on in the marketplace for power tools, and to develop new product ideas." The country managers then give their estimates of how many of the new products they expect to sell— "they're generally not very far out"—and present their marketing plan with any request for more promotional resources.

- **Glaxo,** the UK pharmaceutical group, leaves its national subsidiaries with a high degree of autonomy in the way the group drug portfolio is marketed. It does, however, maintain a small international market development division—part of Glaxo Group Ltd, a central coordinating body headed by a Swiss executive—to act as a repository of experience and to analyze the global market in the broadest sense. It might recommend to subsidiaries how to market a particular product, but, according to one senior executive, "it would be anathema for central marketing to interfere, and if they tried to tell the MDs how to do it, there would be trouble."

for resources. In the development of new products, he will input his needs early on. But his role is changing—now he spends more time thinking about how he can implement corporate global goals."

In the old days, the country managers would have expected to take on special projects themselves, using their own research and manufacturing facilities where appropriate. Now, the business units have the responsibility, and control the research programs in the group laboratories. But some Euro-projects are "missioned out" to individuals or subsidiaries as appropriate. However, developments outside the business units' sphere of influence are in danger of being neglected, leaving the company flat-footed when faced with a competitive challenge in a particular market. New ways are being sought to handle these, and one possibility is the use of "technical centers of excellence" in national companies.

The Matrix Plus

With or without an effective matrix, the search is still on for more effective ways of achieving the great goal of combining local flexibility and initiative with a central strategy. The informal Japanese style or a range of ad hoc solutions can provide answers for some, without committing themselves to the challenge of the network. But the number of alternative structural solutions to the problem of meshing central and local authority is, judging from this survey, relatively small. Most companies, though not all, depend on variants around the theme of geographical managements, aided or limited in some degree by central, product-based departments.

Two companies, 3M and Unilever, have developed structures appropriate to their own special circumstances but noteworthy for their originality and apparent effectiveness, and for the similarity between the solutions they have found. The Unilever organization applies only to its soaps and detergents business, which is much more international in character than frozen food or margarine, but 3M's applies right across the 60,000 product range, save only for products that are so highly specialized (like aircraft weather radar) that no elaborate organization is necessary.

☞ 3M's European management action teams

3M's European structure (see chart page 69) is basically a matrix founded on 17 national subsidiary companies, "the cornerstone of 3M's strength," which report to the regional vice president in Brussels, Edoardo Pieruzzi. Each country manager is responsible for his profits and balance sheet, and is expected to contribute to the group's publicly stated goals of an annual earnings per share growth of 10% or better, return on capital employed of 27% or better and return on equity of 20–25%, with at least 25% of turnover coming from products in existence for less than five years. How the country manager makes up his profit contribution between the company's 60,000 products has not been vital, at least until recently.

Faced with growing international competition in the early 1980s, principally from the Japanese in copiers and photographic materials, 3M gathered its products into around 20 "strategic businesses," each headed by a vice president in the US, to allow product strategies to be developed on a global scale. Before, recalls Pieruzzi, "there were only US strategies adapted for Europe and Japan." The strategic business centers (SBCs) have successfully focused attention on specific product/market nodes, but not all are yet oriented enough toward Europe to satisfy Pieruzzi. Their role is to act as an auditing body, to identify key success factors and to ensure that the lessons are applied on a global scale.

In Europe, some 40 products are now in effect managed by European management action teams (Emats), committees chaired by a product manager from one of the subsidiaries, and comprising manufacturing and technical representatives as well as the general marketing managers from the bigger subsidiaries. The Emats are charged with developing the products' business across Europe, and the chairman reports on progress to the product director in the SBC. Much still depends on how concerned he is in developing the product's European potential, but Pieruzzi finds that "the US management has been forced in general to be much more open to the global approach," and new products are now being developed in Europe to meet European needs.

The Emat thus performs not only the European product management role, but acts as the forum for resolving the normal conflicts arising from the matrix structure. "We now know," says Pieruzzi, "where we're doing a good job and where we're doing a less good job—and the reasons for it." An Emat may nominate a country that has developed a product ahead of the

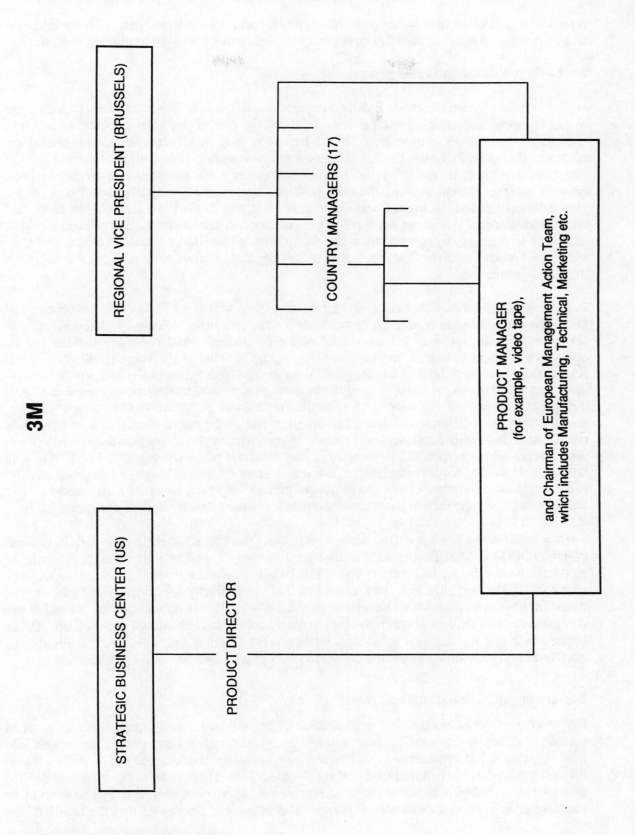

3M

others as a lead subsidiary—France for Scotch Gard and Scotch Brite, the UK for video tape and Post-it Notes etc.—to develop an international advertising and promotional program.

☞ Lever's European brand groups

Unilever began to coordinate its European operations in the late 1960s, before which country managers were responsible for all profits. In 1968, the role of detergents "coordinator" was created, but at a very senior level in the hierarchy and in effect a divisional managing director. Thenceforth, Lever Europe country managers reported for their profits direct to the coordinator. However, there was no mechanism to draw the marketing programs of each country together except through the center. While the present detergents coordinator, Mike Dowdall, has headed the French and German subsidiaries in the past, and has therefore had wide experience of operating across Europe, his London-based central team faced obvious difficulty in pushing, from a distance, the many brands with international potential or "convergence brands" into the European arena. Strictly local brands now account for no more than 20% of turnover.

In early 1990, some key changes were announced (see chart page 71). A chief executive for Lever Europe was appointed to be responsible for the consumer detergents business, including manufacturing. He has his own head office in Brussels, and reporting to him via an operations general manager are the country managers with profit responsibility for each brand. There are six "divisional managers," who are in effect European group product managers, also reporting to the chief executive but through a general manager of strategic management. Each divisional manager is responsible for several European brand groups (EBGs), teams drawn from different countries and based in one of the major markets. Each EBG will consist of a dedicated manager and number of brand managers from "customer" countries, plus market research, product development and financial planning support. The EBGs will now be responsible for developing the marketing strategy, pack design, advertising etc. for Eurobrands and a number of the convergence brands. They will have their own budgets, but will have to "sell" the mix to the customer countries, which are responsible for execution.

Such a split might not appeal to some companies, but the plan is that the EBGs will be effective in the crucial Europewide marketing function as well as in the Emat-style role of reconciling the product and country axes. The fact that the axes are not given formal expression in the Lever organization does not mean that the problem does not exist. Some executives will have split jobs—part European, part local—but that is now common, at least in the companies in this survey. It will help, the company hopes, to break down nationalism. Just as important is that the national subsidiary will preserve its role, and will have the freedom to maneuver and provide ideas for the common good as well as manage its local brands.

Beware organizational mythologies

However well conceived, a neat organization chart with solid and dotted lines and names printed in different sizes suffers one big psychological disadvantage: people are misled into thinking that (a) it represents how the company actually works, and (b) if the reality is different, then the chart should be right, not the managers. There is no suggestion that the 3M or Lever structures suffer unduly in this respect, but in any company, the organization chart can take on a life and a rationale of its own. The managers, conscious that the health of the

LEVER EUROPE

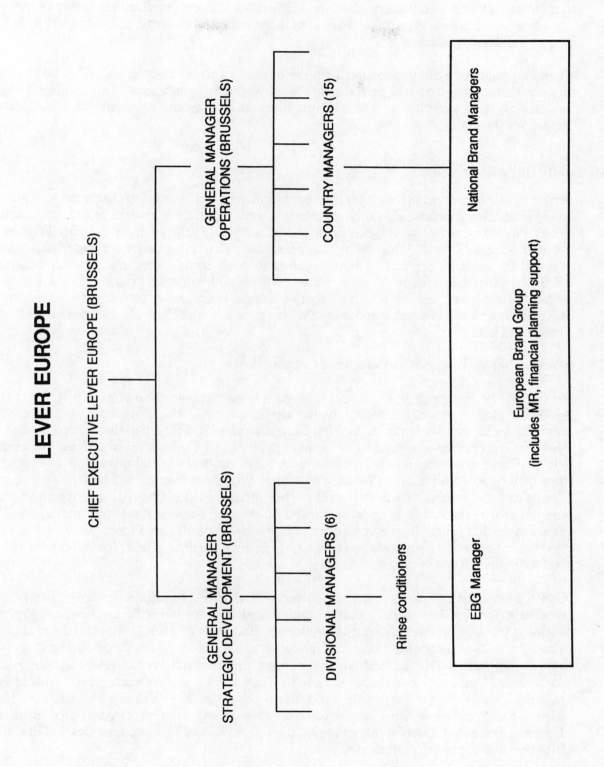

CHIEF EXECUTIVE LEVER EUROPE (BRUSSELS)

GENERAL MANAGER OPERATIONS (BRUSSELS)

COUNTRY MANAGERS (15)

National Brand Managers

GENERAL MANAGER STRATEGIC DEVELOPMENT (BRUSSELS)

DIVISIONAL MANAGERS (6)

Rinse conditioners

EBG Manager

European Brand Group (includes MR, financial planning support) business, not the organization chart, is the key issue, sensibly respond by running it as circumstances and their personalities and inclinations dictate. Intermediate layers of authority are short-circuited, coordinators are kept in the dark and informal links are established to secure the desired outcome.

A more pragmatic policy is to start with the business and the people, and work back to the simplest structures that will help them to work together in harmony. This is the principle underlying the Electrolux and Nestlé structures. It also seems to feature in a number of Japanese companies.

The Japanese Way

An emphasis on performance rather than structural neatness appears to characterize Japanese companies. One Japanese electronics company, which prefers to remain inscrutably anonymous, but with a strong worldwide brand name, is notably relaxed about the coordination of its marketing policies in Europe. The European headquarters does not have executive authority, and the national companies work together through committees, one member of which might be placed in charge of a particular project. Although the company as a whole is organized on functional lines within product groups, cooperation between executives from different functions, like sales and manufacturing, at a tactical level is claimed to be widespread and liberal.

☞ Seeking harmonious structures at Canon

At Canon, the European headquarters is given a rather stronger role (Chapter 3), but it still lacks the clarity which US MNCs would regard as vital. The simplicity of its structure considering its size—it employs 7,000 in Europe alone, 300 of them in the Europa headquarters near Amsterdam—is notable. But Canon prides itself on the level of internal communication. There is a price to pay, however: executives probably spend more time in meetings than their opposite numbers in Western countries. World conferences are held twice a year in Tokyo and last anything up to two weeks. They are attended by the regional executives, the country managers, heads of department and occasionally senior marketing managers. The heads of the big four European countries plus the two factories also meet every two months "to ensure harmony about policy on pricing, marketing, finance, product development and so on," explains European president Takeshi Mitarai.

One Canon country manager calculated recently that, in aggregate, he spent nearly two months a year in liaison and other meetings, and if there is conflict—between, say, the business planning division, covering production and sales of each product, and the country managers—"we compromise in a very Japanese way." A wider purpose of the meetings is to help Canon's central departments in Tokyo, with little experience of anything outside Japan, comprehend marketing conditions in Europe. They are not always successful, and language remains a much bigger barrier for the Japanese than for any Western nation. It is also a barrier for Westerners working in Canon, some of whom feel disconnected from the Japanese grapevine. Despite this problem, there is little doubt that communication in Canon is better than in many Western MNCs.

Canon has learned to its cost the absence of communication in Western companies. One senior Canon director complained, "We licensed some technology to one Western company, and I had to explain one thing to 100 people separately because there was no communication between them. In Canon, if new technology arrives, the information is passed to everyone involved, even to others in different centers." That also applies to its understanding of the market, according to another director, who claimed: "We try to understand the particular demands of different markets. People's requirements and tastes are not the same so we are flexible; we try to find a compromise between countries, and not to force our views on the markets."

Spreading the Load

Whether or not a company has built a formal matrix structure, the need to ensure that country and other senior executives feel part of the European team remains paramount. The issue is not simply one of motivation and enthusiasm. The company needs all the management expertise it can muster in formulating its European, indeed global strategy. The reduction of the middle ranks in the hierarchy, noted earlier, puts greater responsibility on the operational managers to fill the gap and provide a countervailing voice to the central authority. Whether the big decisions are going to be made in Tokyo, Rochester New York or some European center, the European markets have to present a coherent opinion, and the structure must facilitate the deliberation process.

Senior executives, in the words of **IBM**'s market development vice president Elio Catania, "must feel part of the European team." At IBM, country managers at least "share the decisions on a common basis." Catania likes to emphasize that his executives have "two hats—their own country and a Euro-responsibility." Evidently, their concerted view would be difficult for the product divisions back in the US to disregard, just as the individual managers would find it difficult to drag their feet in implementing the majority decision.

For smaller companies, the principle is the same, even if the span of control is rather larger. **Scott Paper,** for example, is directed in Europe by a board consisting of the European president Jack Butler, three managing directors of country groups, plus some worldwide executives. "Each of us," says Butler, "has responsibility for a country plus one important strategic thrust on a regional basis, such as consumer marketing, manufacturing, commercial and industrial, procurement of fiber etc."

☞ Glaxo: coordination and delegation

In 1989, Glaxo established a new coordinating entity, Glaxo Europe Ltd, consisting of the European regional director (resident in Verona, Italy), the directors for the smaller northern and southern countries, and the managing directors of the bigger countries. Glaxo's chairman, Paul Girolami, believes that the formulation of policy should be kept separate from its implementation to ensure that it is not distorted by short-term enthusiasms. As a result, Glaxo Europe acts primarily as a coordinating body between the autonomous national companies and the center. The particular nature of the pharmaceutical industry has driven this process, according to Girolami: "It has very high and risky research expenditure, which must be a central responsibility. On the other hand, clinical trials and the marketing requirements and conditions are highly specific to each country, and the local management must have the freedom to maneuver as circumstances demand."

"We run the group as an integrated business," says Girolami. "Every company relies on other companies for success. We lay down very strict policy rules on what you can say and on quality." But within these guidelines, local managements have extensive autonomy. "The national MD's main job is to lead and monitor performance . . . we can't tell him in London how to do it." For Girolami, the key to establishing an effective groupwide strategy is to respect the human factor: "You've got to motivate people—you don't give orders, you influence them. It's a combination of delegated response guided by central strategy."

In contrast, **Honeywell**'s European policy committee is specifically charged with strategy formulation, although at one stage removed from the US headquarters. Nevertheless, European president Jean-Pierre Rosso is as careful as Girolami about developing local support for corporate decisions: "We spend a lot of time on 'ownership' of strategy. They [the business heads] are buying it in, and if they do, we have a lot less problems." **Heinz**, too, relies on a quarterly steering committee consisting of the three European heads, the European head of Weight Watchers, and Paul Corddry, senior vice president, Europe. Its role is to develop the Heinz pan-European strategy, to monitor progress and "ensure the left hand knows what the right is doing," and to examine three or four current issues in detail.

It would be difficult to run a European operation without regular meetings of the country and product managers in one way or another (in addition to the normal round of planning and budget meetings). But everything depends on the use made of the meetings by the central authority and the members. In one company, the country managers normally meet only once a year, but being in the engineering industry, they may have found that this is adequate for the rate of change. In the computer sector, life is more hectic, and quarterly or even monthly sessions are more usual.

The numbers of country and product managers involved in Europe can make such meetings unwieldy and expensive in executive time unless they are layered. A usual distinction is between the big four markets—UK, France, Germany and Italy—and a wider plenum. But not all companies are equally strong across Europe, and markets where they are still building their presence may demand more input and provide less output in the way of experienced advice than the mature ones.

Developing Teams and Task Forces

Differential development of this kind has encouraged some companies to develop more specialized committees as well as "task forces" to take on specific projects. These frequently cut across the normal departmental boundaries and are an obvious way of tackling many marketing problems. As the need for closer cooperation between national subsidiaries and central product groups grows, this type of response is likely to become more popular. Currently, examples range from Renault's project teams, which aim to speed the development and launch of new models, to Canon's corporate PR group.

☞ **Heinz: No unit is an island**

At Heinz, Corddry prefers bridge-building committees to a coordinating marketing group, which he stresses is not in the corporate culture. As a result, "We've really changed the way we're operating, and you can see the impact elsewhere—the thinking is much less insular."

In addition to the steering committee, Heinz has utilized a series of major task forces to examine specific "prongs of our strategy." Permanent Euro-forums have also been established in each function—marketing, personnel, finance etc.—to share information and determine appropriate action. The chairman of each forum is assigned a specific agenda and "strict marching orders," according to Corddry. One innovation that has already emerged and proved its worth is the "product fair," where the marketing executives from Heinz marketing companies were invited first to the UK to study the market conditions and the products Heinz was marketing there, then to Rome and so on. The purpose is to share experiences and hopefully trigger new ideas.

As a result of all of these consultation exercises, claims Corddry, "When we have met to discuss strategy, and the pressure is put on to apply a foreign solution, it's amazing how easily companies have embraced it, because the executives are wide open to it."

In general, the teamwork approach has a number of advantages:

☐ No extra staff are required, although if these exercises take too much time, the executives' principal duties may be neglected.

☐ Jobs can be distributed through all the subsidiaries to avoid national bias and involve them in the ultimate solutions.

☐ Good use is made of available expertise in the group, and individuals are given valuable multinational experience.

☐ It may be the only effective way of tackling the kind of nebulous, multidepartment problems that afflict many large organizations.

There are considerable drawbacks, however:

☐ Committees, even when given the name task forces or action teams, have an innate tendency to waste executive time—particularly if a lot of traveling is involved—and to get in other people's way.

☐ Their solutions may be difficult to keep track of and control.

☐ They may take longer to find the solution than one executive working full time.

☐ "Forming a committee" is a well-known excuse for inaction.

Tapping the Network Potential

Many of the companies in this report are evidently prepared for the drawbacks, and favor the more flexible, democratic style of management that group working implies. One or two have developed the trend further into "networking," an idea that is rapidly gaining ground, although direct experience of it is still small.

Networking in the management sense has to be distinguished from the information technology meaning, although in practice, the one is made possible only by the other. The broad principle is to rely far less on the conventional hierarchical relationships, and more on informal groupings assembled for specific tasks and ad hoc relationships between individuals.

This is the direction in which Bob Horton, the new chairman of **BP**, is intending to go with his "Project 1990." But Horton recognizes the risks: "There are few examples so far of [networking] having been successful on the scale that we're going to do it."*

However, the old corporate structure had deep-rooted problems that needed to be faced. The central organization was saddled with some 70 central, corporate committees, which Horton regarded as "ridiculous." According to one senior executive, these committees were an indication of a power struggle created by the old matrix structure between the individual businesses and the center. Internal research showed that many senior executives did not know what the company's five-year strategy was, and considered that the corporate structure impeded both operational flexibility and collaboration between businesses. The committees were abolished as one of the first moves of Project 1990.

Another executive admitted: "Control has gone wrong because all of us have concentrated too much on detail. People feel they need to know the answer to every possible question just in case someone asks it. We've lost our way. We need to engender the attitude where I can say 'I can't answer that.'"

Management by fear

The problem of executives surrounding themselves with information and signatures of approval to protect themselves from possible criticism is not peculiar to centralized companies, however, and will not be eliminated by a change of structure, even one as far reaching as Horton plans. It is a problem of management style—of management by fear—which is unlikely to abate unless all the senior executives, from Horton downward, can change their style. As a third senior executive muttered, "Do we *really* think Bob is going to stop second-guessing his top colleagues? That's the only way all this change will work: if the top man behaves differently, managers will take their cue."

Apart from the human and personnel issues of networking (see Chapter 10), a characteristic a number of companies mention is the responsibility placed on the country managers and others to pull out of the center the resources they need—Girolami at Glaxo and Giodano at BOC (see box). The requirement to do this for capital expenditure has long been the practice, and the

---

* *Financial Times*, March 30, 1990.

☞ BOC'S GLOBAL NETWORK

BOC, the UK multinational gases group headed by the American Richard Giodano, is moving toward a global network system of management. He recently explained his company's intentions to the London Business School:

The technology of gas applications is driven by close contact with customers' needs. These applications are often prototyped at our expense at customer locations. Moreover, the customer profile varies considerably from country to country . . . On the other hand, any single gas application usually does have value in more than a few of the countries in which we do business. Finally, the shelf life of these technologies can be as short as one to two years. It is absolutely essential that technology moves from country to country as quickly as possible.

Our organizational solution had to cope with forbidding geography, a wide diversity of technical and operational subject matter, and the involvement of technical and functional personnel as well as general managers. The scale of our businesses simply could not afford local self-sufficiency, nor a traditional managerial pyramid over the whole group driven from the center, nor some form of expensive matrix organization.

Our solution to the problem carries the unimaginative name of "networking." We expect managers and technologists in our group companies throughout the world to take on their shoulders the responsibility for accessing group technology wherever it resides, and to keep appraised of and implement best practices in every aspect of their business.

Our job at the center is to facilitate communication, and occasionally audit. We keep at the center a road map; a written, up-to-date technical inventory, telling us where the technology is and how it works, rather than complete specifications for implementation. We issue publications, sponsor seminars, and create ad hoc short-lived committees to draw our managers' attention to what is available and what is changing. We appoint "lead houses" for specific areas of technology or operational problems. A lead house could be in Sydney or Osaka, but it would be identified as the most knowledgeable within our group on that subject. It would have special responsibilities for dissemination of that knowledge to other group members round the world. We don't expect its work to be duplicated by other group companies.

Networking is fast, efficient, but not so easy to sustain. It requires that managers live with more than average ambiguity and sometimes conflicting objectives. Networking implies giving and taking. Individuals are often called upon for contributions that have no immediate benefit to their P&L.

Networking implies a high degree of cooperation and trust rather than authority . . . Our organization also recognizes that there is no single source of wisdom in the group. Networking values speed and flexibility. Above all else, it recognizes that delay is costly and often fatal . . . The biggest challenge we face in exploiting the full potential of networking is cultural. The forging of an Anglo-American management culture was relatively easy compared to the task we now face in achieving that same result with our Far Eastern associates.

procedure for justifying capital and other projects is well established. Not so common is the extension of the principle to technical, marketing and sales support, the rationale being:

- subsidiaries are much more likely to use resources effectively if they can call for the support themselves rather than have it thrust down their throats;

- poor performance cannot be blamed on inappropriate central policies;

- in order to win individual battles in the global war, small subsidiaries must be encouraged to call on group resources even though their own cash flows could not support the investment.

Once again, much depends on the cultural atmosphere. If blame, recrimination and a paranoic anxiety to be associated only with success are the prevailing executive characteristics, no structural device will have much effect. But networking offers some prospect of making cooperation and the deployment of ideas and expertise more effective because:

- communication is quicker, less formal and not confined to the "proper channels";

- a network extends horizontally as well as vertically, across departmental boundaries and national frontiers—junior marketing executives in subsidiary A might talk direct to senior service managers in subsidiary C or D to solve a particular problem, rather than only (and if at all) through the center;

- these links are not dependent on the limited "exchange capacity" at the center, in terms either of the volume of traffic, or imagination and responsiveness to new ideas.

The network idea has been taken up enthusiastically in some academic circles, partly because it does promise some practical means of reconciling central authority with local autonomy—and perhaps also because of a natural academic empathy with its egalitarian, anti-hierarchical characteristics. Nevertheless, the problems that networking poses should not be underestimated:

- The primary purpose of a structure is to facilitate effective action toward a centrally determined objective. In a crisis, a network might well impede that process.

- Drive and commitment in the organization can quickly be lost if there is no obvious center of authority. The geographical identity of the center has a powerful psychological impact.

- A network depends on a much better accounting and information technology system than even the most advanced companies have yet installed (see Chapter 9). The cost of such a system for a major MNC can run into hundreds of millions of dollars.

- A network depends on a degree of maturity and expertise among executives that may take some time to emerge.

- There is little practical experience to draw on: none of the companies in this report has developed networking to any significant degree, nor has the system had to face periods of radical change or crisis.

The spirit of the times

Despite these disadvantages and criticisms, networking goes with the grain of current developments in corporate organization. Companies anxious to make the best use of scarce and increasingly expensive talent are likely to experiment with networks in some degree, even if the conventional structure is retained in the background.

Part III

Scale and Diversity

Chapter 8
Targeting Sales and Prices

Whatever companies conclude about the proper location and structure of their marketing operations, there is no such controversy over sales. The need to keep close to the customers, and to put as much decision-making power as possible into the hands of the executives in contact with them, ensures that sales will remain a fundamentally local operation. That does not necessarily mean that local salesmen deal only with local business, or that the bulk of the business will remain local; only that whereas marketing is primarily about strategy, and therefore needs to be in a position to scan distant horizons, selling is essentially tactical, and always depends on local, practical contact, however and wherever the customer is organized. The sales structure must therefore reflect that fact.

Yet selling in the European context evidently presents multinational companies with a problem similar to marketing: with a growing proportion of cross-border and international business, how should the sales force be organized to:

- provide the close attention to local customers that they demand;

- coordinate its actions with company sales teams in other countries to provide a coherent service to cross-border customers;

- utilize its reputation with a customer in one country to assist the development of sales to that customer elsewhere;

- concentrate, develop and deploy corporate expertise in solving customers' problems;

- service effectively the small but growing volume of essentially international business, whether from retailers' buying groups or international services like credit card operators and airline booking systems;

- mount an effective "instant response" to unexpected business opportunities that do not fit the company's existing organization;

- set prices that meet the demands of the local market while relating to the wider European context.

Few companies claim to be satisfied with the organization that they so far have in place to meet these objectives, and admit to having made mistakes in the past when they tried to tackle the issues too enthusiastically. Ten years ago, the Swedish paper and packaging company **ASSI** experimented with cross-border selling to its carton manufacturers in an

THE PUBLIC PROCUREMENT CHALLENGE

Organizing an effective sales response to the increasing number of lucrative public contracts open to competitive tender is becoming a major competitive issue for companies. Decisions have to be made about whether the particular national subsidiary is going to handle it, or whether the local resources are inadequate for the task and some other solution needs to be found. With companies' determination to keep central staff to a minimum, the only way forward may be to pull some of the expertise of the bigger national subsidiaries into a task force—assuming that the appropriate networking facilities are in place.

This issue will become more pressing following the EC agreement to liberalize public procurement contracts as part of the Internal Market Program. From 1990, some public-sector contracts will be open to the cheapest or "the most economically advantageous" tender from anywhere in the EC. From January 1, 1993, all contracts for energy, transportation, water and telecommunications projects will be open to any supplier in the EC; these areas are currently excluded from the EC's procurement rules, even though they account for half of public-sector purchasing. Also from 1993, private-sector monopoly or quasi-public-sector contracts above a minimum size will be included.

The result is that about 50,000 big contracts will be open to competition every year. Advertisements inviting tenders will be published in the Official Journal of the European Communities, and will also be available on the Tenders Economic Daily electronic database. The aim is to open a huge seam of EC business to cross-border competition, rather than allow member states to reserve their own contracts for domestic suppliers. How effective the regulations will be in ensuring open competition can only be guessed at, and no one expects protectionist instincts to disappear overnight. But there is little doubt that the new rules will produce an explosion of new activity among potential suppliers of all sorts and sizes for contracts, from consultancy services and office cleaning to power stations and telephone exchanges.

Interested companies will have to assess the most effective way of selecting which potential contracts to tender for and how to handle the ensuing preparation work. Central monitoring of the contract advertisements could be necessary, but certainly the smaller contracts will be left to the national subsidiaries—or to a nominated subsidiary where the company has no suitable base. Bigger, possibly multinational, contracts raise wider organizational issues over how far the center is willing and able to pull together all the business units and national subsidiaries to make a viable bid, or even to negotiate a joint venture to strengthen its position quickly in a particular market.

In some industries, the developments in Brussels are simply extending an area of large-scale one-off business that has been increasing in significance for some time. Big international projects like the Amadeus airline reservation system do not often fit neatly into the company's existing structure, and **IBM** has found it necessary to set up what it calls its "Opportunity Management System" as a means of ensuring that this sort of contract does not slip through its fingers. IBM describes this as a "bottom-up reporting mechanism which allows us to identify the most promising opportunities that require a common European investment, where the best thing might be a central European team to package the solution." But the emphasis, in IBM's new decentralized mode, is that such activities are inspired from the field, not thrust down from above.

attempt to cut costs, but quickly found that "it didn't work very well," and ever since has maintained national sales forces. That appears to be the pattern for most companies in this report, and looks likely to continue at least for the next five years, although some executives foresee possible adjustments of boundaries. This could mean, for example, Bavaria and Austria being treated as one administrative unit, and Belgium being divided according to language. Generally, however, customer sensitivity is going to be accorded a higher priority than bureaucratic convenience.

The situation changes when customers themselves spread across borders and demand a similar service on both sides. At **Kodak,** for example, "we all think the general corporate structure [which includes national sales forces controlled ultimately by the country managers] is now about right." But there is a tacit acknowledgement that the multinational client problem, although still small in relation to the total business, has not yet been solved. **Canon,** however, is relaxed about its solution. It finds that "some customers want a special relationship worldwide, even a worldwide contract but with local distribution and service, and so we need more coordination. And if countries really come together after 1992, we shall need some new structures—but we can do it at any time."

Connecting in to the Matrix

Being locally based, most sales forces have been the direct line responsibility of the country manager, and have in effect provided his power base in the organization (unless he has manufacturing responsibilities as well). Nothing happens, as salesmen are fond of saying, until somebody sells something, and the vital importance of maintaining sales volume is what makes many companies cautious in tinkering with the organization. But as they have been placing more emphasis on planning and coordinating their marketing across Europe, the salesmen as well as the marketing staff are faced with more ambiguous reporting relationships.

At a minimum, Danish toy company **Lego** has adopted a central sales liaison group to coordinate its operations. Headed by a senior European sales vice president, it consists of a number of junior liaison officers representing the center in each country, and the countries at the center. Generally, the country manager is still the boss on matters to do with sales targets and their achievement, but the way these are achieved and the direction of the sales team to target customers and market segments are increasingly the concern of business units, product directors etc. taking a Europewide view.

Bringing the two together is not always easy. **Union Carbide,** for one, has found in its gases division that communication between the field and the central marketing operation in Geneva has not been good enough. Apparently, its salesmen can see marketing as a diversion. In consequence, a marketing manager "with sales experience" is being appointed in each sales subsidiary to act as an intelligence officer, gathering information about the market and feeding it back to Geneva.

Where companies already have critical mass in a country, with sufficient cash flow to cover the overheads, they can afford a more detailed coverage of the market, as the following SKF example shows.

☞ SKF: Fine-tuning sales success

In the major reorganization of SKF (see Chapter 4), the old functional structure with domestic sales, international sales, manufacturing, finance etc. was replaced by global product divisions within a "business area." Thus Bearing Industries is divided into the automotive division (the biggest, but with a very few, very large customers), machinery and some smaller divisions, all with a lot of smaller customers. In the major national markets, each division maintains profit-responsible business units within the national company. Sales, however, remains a local responsibility, with budgets and targets set locally but agreed with the product divisions.

Explains marketing director Anders Braennstroem, "We have the resources here centrally to initiate and lead the work, and to follow it up. We do not have the resources to undertake the task in the field." Braennstroem explains that issues such as product specification and design are developed for customers in particular market segments. The system is in a state of constant evolution: "We're always fine-tuning it," says Braennstroem. "The reasons why it works or doesn't are in many cases a question of fine-tuning. Where are the resources, where is the knowledge; are those with the knowledge really doing the work?"

In the rather static light bulb industry, the Siemens-owned **Osram** has enjoyed a unified product range across Europe ever since the establishment in 1927 of the Phoenix cartel, which set price and product standards among other things. That has long since been abolished, but the standardization largely endures. Even so, per capita consumption of light bulbs varies by a factor of more than five from one end of Europe to another, and distribution conditions are equally diverse. Because inflation in one country is much higher than in another, wholesalers' priorities in holding stock are widely different, and in some countries, retailers' brands account for a large share of the market. The sales operation remains highly localized therefore, whereas product management is highly centralized in Munich, and the Osram brand identity is heavily promoted internationally.

There is an obvious distinction to be drawn between the consumer goods sales executive calling on wholesale and retail buyers to offer standard products like light bulbs or detergents, and the industrial equipment representative hoping to apply corporate expertise and technology to a customer's problem. What the sales executives offer in both cases will generally be a mix of international and local products. But success in modern markets demands that they and their companies draw on marketing and technical expertise stored either at the center or somewhere else in the network, and rigorously apply it according to a centrally agreed strategy.

Roche, for example, sees that the big food groups, customers for its vitamins, flavors and fragrances, will eventually have one central buying unit for the whole of Europe. Roche will therefore have to build "Eurosales teams" to deal with one central organization. It will place bigger orders and make more sophisticated demands which the teams will have to develop the expertise to meet. The company structure becomes the delivery mechanism. If the plans of Associated Marketing Services (see Chapter 2) for the food industry become a reality, food manufacturers will have to act sooner rather than later to take a European view of their business. AMS members already account for 12,000 stores supplying an average of 11% of total grocery sales in nine EC and Efta countries. The costs and the benefits of doing business with AMS are therefore a prime corporate issue.

Selling Across Frontiers

The growing number of multinational customers is likely to exacerbate the inherent conflict between the need to satisfy local customers and the need to take a global view. Most companies still buy locally, but as Canon has foreseen, there may be a need to coordinate sales operations across several countries—with the inevitable penalty to pay in a restriction of the local freedom to do a deal. The volume or other discounts offered, special terms, credit allowed and service levels may all be affected, and demand not only some degree of uniformity but a great deal of communication between subsidiaries to put together a viable package and work out how the costs will be shared.

The advantage, of course, is that the company can use its existing business with a company in one country as a means of developing opportunities in another. However, it is a tactic likely to be effective only if communication between the two subsidiaries is at least as good as communication inside the potential customer. Bad news can travel faster than good, and if the customer is dissatisfied in Munich, it is unlikely to be very receptive in Manchester or Madrid. In these circumstances, greater responsibility is placed on the sales and other staff handling the business in one country, both to do a good job and to pass along useful information to help colleagues elsewhere do the same. The problem arises as to how this process should be managed, without merely adding to central staffing levels.

The lead country solution

The simple solution is to nominate as lead country the national subsidiary with the biggest stake in the business, the most knowledge of it, or just the one in whose territory the customer's head office is located. The country manager of the lead country is made ultimately responsible for the development of the worldwide business with a particular customer. The other subsidiaries then have to liaise with him before making a significant move. This is the system IBM has just introduced (see Chapter 5). Another, well-established example is TI John Crane, the Dutch subsidiary of which has Shell as its international customer. Thanks to Crane's information system (see Chapter 8), it can keep a running check on the business the account is yielding. Companies that still cannot aggregate their sales and profit data across countries by product, market segment or customer are at a clear disadvantage.

Crane is satisfied with its system, but in other sorts of business and corporate cultures the familiar problems of conflicting loyalties and motivation may arise. If the company is not prepared for them, internal turf battles may be fought more strenuously than those with its competitors:

☐ Will the lead country be successful in persuading its fellows to put as much urgency behind satisfying its own customer's foreign offshoots as they would their major accounts?

☐ If a lot of effort is involved to win the business, should the subsidiaries spend their time on that rather than on their own, perhaps hotter prospects?

☐ If money is involved, who pays, and who receives the ultimate commission or bonus?

As the volume of cross-border business grows, therefore, a more formal procedure for dealing with these problems may be necessary. **Rank Xerox** designates account managers in lead countries who are paid a small commission on sales to their accounts made outside their territory. Such business is still relatively rare, says a Rank Xerox executive. It has only 30 or 40 such accounts at the moment, "but we're now adding 20 or so a year. We can't go faster than the customers want us to." Some want a consistent price across the world, while others want to transfer special systems to other centers. American Express, for one example, uses Xerox technology to produce reduced copies of all its transaction chits, which it wanted to bring to Europe. It talked to its US account manager, who passed the matter on to a small coordination team in the European headquarters, which passed it on to the UK account manager. It may be long-winded, but if American Express is satisfied—as we shall see, it has its own coordination problems, possibly over companies like Rank Xerox—the process is worth it.

At **Honeywell**, some 50 account managers are deployed worldwide to deal with its big multinational customers. They are essentially an extension of the subsidiary and are based near the customer's head office. The account manager for Shell happens to be Finnish, and lives in Brussels. The local subsidiary takes responsibility for building the business, but, explains European president Jean-Pierre Rosso, "if the affiliate wants to cut 15% to get the business, the account manager may say no because of the worldwide implications. The business unit has to be linked in, and the account manager gets at least as much guidance from there as from the affiliate." If it turns out that a small subsidiary has to shoulder heavy costs to support account managers, a cost-sharing system comes into effect.

Compaq makes use of its small, Munich-based central marketing department to perform a similar function. Many of its 20–30 staff are in fact based in the subsidiaries, and their role is to support rather than lead. Once again, Shell is one of their targets, particularly after Shell's US operation "bought thousands" of Compaq PCs early in the computer company's development, according to one senior executive. Compaq in the Netherlands therefore had to make certain that its credentials were known and understood at Shell's Dutch headquarters in the Hague, and that the Dutch subsidiary could offer the same (or a better) level of service as its US counterpart.

"You can't operate in one market without having a potential effect on the others," says a senior executive. "Each market has its own qualities and distinctions which we must utilize but still remain consistent in our message, terms and conditions etc. Hopefully, we achieve the right balance." One new development Compaq is now encountering is the growing number of its dealers, including the US chain Businessland but also some from the UK, that are building networks in other European countries—underlining the virtue of Compaq's original insistence on standard terms and conditions for its dealers worldwide.

Selling Services

The service industries often represent a more complex problem in that standards are less easily defined and interconnections more important. Advertising agencies, for example, have developed international chains of offices to serve their multinational and other clients, some of which rely on them to provide a coordinated service to subsidiaries in a number of countries. Others work differently. Consultant Tim Breene complains that agency WCRS (before its restructuring) had "one set of clients (like Unilever or United Distillers) that were internationalizing, and another set that were not, and we had to organize for both." For the former, WCRS relied on a lead agency to be the custodian of advertising quality, strategy, development etc. for an international account, which the other agencies in the group had to follow under the eye of a small, high-caliber team at the center.

Even so, satisfying a client in each country, whether in the interpretation of the advertising ideas or in other aspects of account servicing such as media buying, billing etc., is not easy, and most of the big agencies suffer from a wide variation in the standard of service they can offer in their international networks. Some, like WPP, owner of the J Walter Thompson and Ogilvy & Mather chains (and a host of smaller marketing services firms), reckons to find at least 15% of its new business from "cross referrals," i.e. inquiries fielded elsewhere in the group. However, there is a continuing debate among advertisers—a variation, in fact, of the global/local theme—about whether they benefit more from a coordinated service from an international agency, or from selecting the best agency for their purpose in each market.

☞ **Defining lines of communication at Amex**

More detailed integration is required for charge cards, which are used increasingly internationally by their holders. One part of American Express's sales program is directed toward its "service establishments" (SEs), the retailers, hotels, oil companies' gas station chains etc. that accept the card; the other part to major employers that issue the cards to their staff. (Selling to the consumer is carried out largely by advertising and direct marketing, handled round the world by Ogilvy & Mather and McCann-Erickson.) But both the SEs and employers have cross-border operations which Amex takes into account when calculating charges.

The implication, explains UK managing director Alan Stark, is that "there need to be a lot of lines of communication. You have to define exactly who does what." The national subsidiaries look after all SEs based in their territories and employers issuing less than 10,000 cards. The London-based European headquarters handles the large employers and the international marketing for the SEs. Employers are given a discount based on the total number of cards they issue but paid in local currency, although some may be offered a dollar price. The sales forces therefore have to network information on companies with foreign offshoots promptly and accurately, and groups specializing in, say, hotels or airlines meet regularly to coordinate sales programs and conditions, and unravel the problems.

Setting the Price

Of all the issues raised by the coalescence of the European markets, pricing was singled out by several companies in the survey as their biggest single headache. Partly this is a reflection of the economic disparities within the European Community and the gray market problems that arise when prices are too far out of line between countries. Partly also, pricing is the litmus test of the company's management system. Local autonomy means nothing if prices are set centrally; conversely, if the need to coordinate prices throughout Europe is the overriding factor, how does the company give its product divisions and national subsidiaries the decision-making autonomy that good customer service demands?

The problem is made worse by mounting public awareness of the price differences. Auto manufacturers, as already noted, are under scrutiny over the substantial price differentials they manage to maintain between neighboring countries. That may be one reason why their pricing decisions are generally centralized, as Claude Lacelle, director of commercial planning at Renault, explains:

> It's not the people in Austria or Spain, for example, who set their prices. On the basis of information they give us, we make proposals on pricing for new models or for price increases—according to a well-defined methodology which is the same for all countries—and submit them to the finance division. And we try to make our price proposals a good compromise between competitiveness and profitability . . . Our standard policy would be to compare a new model with the competition in the country concerned. We have data on products, prices and sales performance, so we can say we'll position ourselves here, here or here.

IBM is in the process of restructuring its pricing policies at the moment, but is not yet ready to reveal how its twin aims of harmonization and flexibility at the country level will be achieved. Its rival NCR says that it "prices to the local market, but we have to come up with multinational strategies through discounts. We'll be moving toward a single price structure, but we've got to give flexibility to local managers. What's happening is that local pricing is becoming very similar, the UK being one of the lowest in Europe, with several countries like Italy and Germany easing downward."

The pressure for comparable pricing in different European markets will hit margins, which explains some of the manufacturers' reluctance to change. But taking the initiative in a desirable direction may be preferable. **L'Oréal**, for example, with its generally decentralized structure, recognizes that across its range of hair care, perfume and pharmaceutical products, prices have been coming together for several years. Therefore, in the past five years, "harmonization has been speeded up deliberately—but by consensus . . . Prices are decided according to common denominators of concept, product technique and method of use by the consumer, and position in the local market. For modern products, price levels are becoming more uniform. There's a good example, Studio Line, a brand which is absolutely the same in 40 different countries . . . in terms of packaging, product technique and price level."

Problems can arise not just with fluctuations in the exchange rates, but with discounts, credit terms, ordering patterns, delivery conditions etc., all of which affect the margin finally made, but all of which have to be negotiated locally. John Ankeny, Levi Strauss's European marketing services director, expects to see a move to a common price for Levi jeans over the next two years, and he already charges his national subsidiaries a standard transfer price. But in the fashion trade, discounts can vary in bizarre ways, and "I don't even want to know."

Matching the competition

In industrial markets, where multinational customers are slowly learning to buy the goods in whichever country the price is lowest, there is some urgency in closing the gaps, at least to within tolerable limits. At one engineering company, the pricing strategy is reviewed across Europe every year, and thereafter, "we're happy if national subsidiaries operate within plus or minus 12%. That absorbs exchange rate wobbles, and is below the pain threshold of major customers."

Other companies, however, may have to pay rather more attention to their competitors, some of which may be in no way inhibited by European pricing strategies. **Compaq** has just introduced a range of PCs to compete with the down-market Far Eastern competition in many of its territories, but its main preoccupation is IBM, whose prices it uses as a marker. "Sometimes we're higher than IBM," it reports, "and we avoid positioning ourselves underneath." Rank Xerox issues pricing guidelines from the center, which it intends should keep its products within 10% of key competitors and yield a 50–60% gross margin. The subsidiaries "only come back to us if they can't meet the guidelines—if, for example, competitive prices are too low."

The risk is, of course, that two rivals following that policy can chase each other down the price spiral. The consequences of getting the price structure wrong in that or other ways can be serious, and will become more so as customers take more interest in differences. The need for up-to-date, accurate and internationally comparable data is therefore growing fast, in this area as elsewhere. The implications are examined in the next chapter.

Chapter 9

Keeping Control: the Impact of Information Technology

Controlling and coordinating European operations demand better and more detailed information systems than most companies have at present. Modern information technology systems promise major benefits, but only to those who are prepared to adapt their structures to match and who have thought through its fundamental purpose.

Decentralization, matrix structures, task forces and networks all depend in a very intimate way on the corporate control system, the flow of management information and, increasingly, the potential of IT. The UK-based **Oasis** consultancy, established by Robb Wilmott, regards information, organization and strategy as the three corners of a corporate triangle. The failure of any one of these three elements will thwart the success of the other two. Other consultants make the point that their clients frequently fail to appreciate the distorting effect their control systems can have on the progress of the business.

That has always been the case, and there are probably few companies whose controls have adequately kept pace with or anticipated the development of the business. But the evolution of a modern European structure, with its delicate balance of central and local authority demands a parallel development in information systems. Team working and networking, in particular, assume that all members have ready access to the data they need and can communicate efficiently with each other. The implications of that assumption are enormous. One multinational client of Oasis in the petrochemical industry is in the midst of a four-year program costing hundreds of millions of dollars to implement 18 major information systems in 16 countries.

The evidence from this report suggests that many other companies will be forced to make a thorough overhaul of their control and information systems. **Electrolux** is well on the way. Its "Electrolux Forecasting & Supply" system is linking some 70 appliance companies in 13 European countries with an IT network. Ultimately, all manufacturing, supply and marketing operations will be provided with real-time data on production, sales, stocks and market activity. As a senior financial executive points out, "With the large number of companies we have, to control them, we must have a uniform reporting system which is correct and tells us how the company is doing."

What Information?

The crucial issue is what information the system should carry, and, behind that, what sort of control the company wishes to exercise. The role of the center in respect of its subsidiaries has already been discussed (see Chapter 3). In its judgment of a subsidiary's performance, central management has to decide:

☐ Whether it is able, or obliged, to accept a country manager's or divisional director's view on how well the operation is doing.

☐ Or whether it needs to come to its own conclusion based on the information supplied, or judged against other similar operations or some external source.

☐ What action it needs to take if the results are not up to expectations.

For **3M,** one of the merits of the Emat system (see Chapter 7) is that it provides a means of judging a subsidiary's performance for a particular product, but only because the team is able to draw the data together and, on the basis of its own experience, compare one country with another. In the view of Marcus Alexander of London-based consultants **GAH,** the basic control system should help to do that by providing local managers with the ability to see the advantage of being part of the greater whole, the incentive to draw on its strengths, and the opportunity to do so.

Alexander cites the case of a retail group which decided to make each store manager responsible for profit. "The initial reaction was to cut things that could influence the result. But the brighter managers started to pull resources out of head office to help them increase their profit."

Systems analysts expect managers to be able to specify the data they need to do their jobs, but that is rarely the case, particularly in a fast-changing business. Historical financial information is one thing; "soft" order totals, sales activity, market trend and economic information etc. are quite another. As the report *From Hierarchy to Network* published by the Conference Board Europe warns:

> The availability of information makes it tempting for senior managers to bypass or invade the territories of their subordinates. This can feel like lack of trust. We have always to be clear why we need to dispense information: are we telling, counting or trusting? It has to be clear to all concerned. One study in one organization discovered that 40% of its information costs were due only to the need for reassurance at the top.

Japanese companies' very detailed but informal system of reporting has the advantage of not being rigid and specific in the manner of some Western companies. The Doyle study (see Chapter 4) on subsidiaries operating in the UK concluded:

> The Americans relied much more on detailed and formal controls. Most employed standard planning and budgeting systems, and reported to international product and marketing committees. . . . The Japanese did not favor the standardized planning systems; instead they relied on continuous informal monitoring. All subsidiaries indicated that reporting was a daily or constant process, with the tele-

phone as the main mode of communication with Japan. Headquarters were invariably viewed as extremely well informed of activities, problems and progress.

US and UK companies, Doyle concluded, focused on financial measures such as budgeted profit and return on investment targets, and did not monitor performance at the market or product-line level—giving, in his view, an inevitably short-term flavor to their policies. Japanese firms were more concerned with market share targets and strategy, and local managers knew the company was committed to long-term growth. Judging from the companies included in this report, it is doubtful whether such strictures could be applied to 3M or even IBM, in spite of the strong emphasis on profit, but the effect of control systems on the way the company's structure operates and develops is not in doubt.

As companies widen their focus beyond their national subsidiaries, and coordinate their marketing and sales activities whether through product divisions or in other ways, the control system has to change also. Taking a global view on some or all of the products requires global information on them. Subsidiaries frequently still do not analyze their profits by product line, and even where they do, accounting differences sometimes make it difficult to relate the Italian figure to the French or Swedish. But without accurate data of that kind, an issue can be judged at national level only according to national profit criteria, and cannot be isolated from national overheads. Therefore, the central product manager or director can assume only an advisory role, and must leave the ultimate decision to the country manager.

Collecting the Data

"To get an accurate assessment of marketing costs is a particularly thorny issue," finds Oasis consultant Mike Perkin. "Systems have usually grown up on accounting lines and are therefore transaction oriented. You're calling for a company to make a major departure on centralized accounting to view the operation on functional, vertical market lines." Rather than adapt the existing system, some companies have decided to scrap it and start again, with all the risks and expense that that entails—hence the major expenditure by one of the oil companies referred to above.

"All nationalities work differently, so when you operate in so many different countries, it's not just the systems that have to change but the way you take an order, handle stock, and run the distribution and accounts," says Perkin. When setting up a new operation like Chep's pallet hire in Germany, such details can be made universal from the start. Compaq was also careful to adopt common terms and conditions for its computer dealers right round the world, including discounts, payment terms and promotional expenditure. It has faced problems with some big dealers, but an important benefit is that data are comparable from Minneapolis to Madrid. The lack of comparability can be a major obstacle. As one senior Colgate-Palmolive executive found in the early 1980s, "We couldn't make any sense out of the data we had. For a given product line, it was collected and analyzed in countries all around the world under different assumptions and with different methods."

There is an accompanying risk. For the system to accommodate every oddity in every country, it has to be comprehensive, and can become too clumsy and time consuming for the operators, who will then short-circuit it if they can. On the other hand, simplification may conceal the very differences that spell success or failure. Market research information, in particular, is notoriously difficult to relate from one country to another, partly for reasons of demography, partly methodology. But some US MNCs' attempts to impose their own research methodology on, for example, advertising effectiveness have not been noticeably more effective. That is one important reason for retaining local management with enough skill to interpret the data and enough authority to adapt or even abandon the rules when the occasion demands.

At **Black & Decker,** European chief Roger Thomas finds that "asking subsidiaries for more sales is a waste of time," partly because they are already well motivated to sell as much as the trade will bear, but partly too because "you can also 'buy' forward sales with discounts. So we measure sales out (from the retailers), not sales in, and the pipeline stock." Those data are harder to collect, but the company has had many years experience of assessing the level of retail sales from the number of guarantee cards that customers return, and basing its production programs on them rather than its own invoiced sales.

One industrial company that claims to have an effective, bottom-up management information system in place is **John Crane,** part of the UK engineering company, TI Group. Crane has 60,000 items on its product list—seals for all sorts of moving machinery—and its national subsidiaries all use common software which details sales, prices, costs etc. by product. "We roll up performance with each major customer weekly and monthly," says a senior central executive. "If margins are too low, perhaps because of discounts, we can take action."

Like several other companies, Crane is also using a common computer-aided design (CAD) system to stimulate the generation of new ideas throughout the group, simplify and speed their development, and prevent duplication. Like many companies, Crane is concerned to increase the rate of innovation and throughput without adding staff, whether in the subsidiaries or the center. Modern technology offers the prospect of whisking design proposals, draft specifications, costings and almost any quantity of accompanying data to wherever in the world it is needed. **Thorn EMI**'s lighting division, before its aborted sale to GTE of the US, was planning to spend £20 million on upgrading its CAD/CAM system over the next few years so that, for example, an architect in Milan could specify the product design, which would then be made in Germany or the UK. "We have the computing power to do it now, but it's not yet good enough," commented an executive. As in other companies, such a system will be effective only if common standards are in force in technical, financial and operational terms.

In management terms, such systems have a two-way effect: the center is able to keep in much closer contact with conditions at the battle front, and the local sales and marketing executives are provided with precise and up-to-date information about pricing estimates, deliveries, the feasibility of variants etc. Providing salesmen with lap-top or hand-held computers has a similar effect. Some of **Lego**'s toy salesmen have been using hand-held computers for some years to collect and record retailers' order levels, sales and stocks. The information can then be processed by the subsidiary and fed into the central computers to provide a more detailed and immediate picture of sales trends than would be feasible in other ways.

Carefully planned, such systems can also give the salesman much more authority when talking to customers. In a case in which Oasis consultant Mike Perkin was recently involved,

"The salesman can be thousands of miles away but is given a clear picture of prices, credit limits and other details. That represents a significant increase in delegated authority, but it demands that the price-setting process and the rules for establishing the high and low limits have to be clear and widely understood." Decision making can thus be pushed right down the line and literally next to the customer, and intermediate executive layers avoided. For the system to be effective, the center must be well prepared with a thoroughly researched strategy and the necessary expertise to apply it, and the salesmen well trained as to the exercise of their power and the limits of their competence. But the benefits to the customer in terms of prompt and accurate quotations or delivery dates are obvious.

Believing the Data

It is a fact of corporate life that the information submitted by subsidiaries to headquarters will reflect the expectations, and the bonuses, attached to it. If the center believes that service engineers should make a minimum of five calls per day or that debtors be cut to an average 60 days, that is what, within three months or so, the data will actually show. If a bonus depends on it, the period will be reduced by a month. That may seem too cynical, but dishonesty is not necessarily implied: the basic facts, or the way the data are collected, are often open to interpretation, and it is only human nature to interpret them in the most favorable way if a lot hangs on the outcome. The underlying reality may be different.

The problem extends beyond information. One executive with long experience at a big multinational remarks: "If you want to apply a policy to 20 subsidiaries, some will be simply incompetent, others will not do as they are told." The more the center tries to "manage" its subsidiaries and draw them in to a global strategy, the worse the problem could become. "Once the basic belief in a control system breaks down, you're in a mess," warns GAH consultant Marcus Alexander, who sees one solution to lie in giving subsidiaries the obligation to pull the resources they need from the center, rather as Glaxo does. In that way, the prized global strategy may not be so neat and tidy, and progress may be a bit slower, but at least the center will have more confidence that apparent progress is real.

No companies in the report admitted to difficulties of this kind—it would be surprising if they did, and quite possible that they were unaware that they existed. But several companies emphasized the importance of trust in a complex international structure, principally between individuals but also in the data and research that they produce. **Colgate-Palmolive**'s European president, Brian Bergin, for example, affirms that "in a changing European environment, integrity is very important. There's a lot of game playing in any organization, but it has to be minimized, and data mustn't be used as an excuse for the differences between markets." One of his solutions is to make sure that executives do not lose touch with their markets, and get out into the field at least once a week. Other companies have stressed the importance of their senior executives knowing each other and having worked together over a long period.

Data and the Network

As companies move toward more lateral and flexible structures, the data availability and flow become of critical importance. The problem that strikes many is that the existing information flow is primarily vertical—from sales branches and warehouses to regional offices to national offices to European offices and to headquarters. Differences in definitions or accounting standards may be accommodated as the data are consolidated, and the totals stored in the central data banks, usually in a form to suit the accounts department.

More flexible marketing structures may therefore demand radical change in information systems, particularly if the company is aiming to allow executives access to sales and marketing data across the group. The growing use of personal computers and work stations connected into local area networks potentially allows every executive to pull out the information needed from any part of the company, work on it, send the result to the other members of a task force in three different countries for further work and modification, then implement the agreed result. It is a tempting vision, but the survey shows how much work needs to be done to reach that state.

Even a company as sophisticated in data handling as **NCR** admits that its present management information system is inadequate for its future purposes. Says senior European vice president Fred Newall, "We need common support systems because it eliminates problems of discussion. We've tried in the past to adjust to local systems, but now we're evolving our administration along open Unix system lines. At the moment, national companies can talk to each other, but on a hierarchical basis, and there's no peer-to-peer communication." A lot is achieved at NCR, claims Newall, by informal networks of people who have had long experience in the company and know how it works. He gained his knowledge when he spent a year acting as executive assistant to the chairman and president.

The systems problems that NCR faces are widespread. **Colgate-Palmolive**, for example, has realized the need for major changes. Says European president Brian Bergin: "We have to rewire all our operations, between departments and across Europe—they all tend to be vertical. It's difficult to overestimate the need for data bases. I'm appalled how far we've got to go." A further complication in his case is that Europe has to link in to the US and the rest of the world. Ideally, a uniform, global system might be the right goal, but the additional complexities that would be entailed would possibly not justify the cost.

Making the world smaller

US computer manufacturer **Digital Equipment** claims that it has been networking internally for the past 10 years, backing its detailed matrix management system. Of its present 124,000 employees (a cut of 6,000 is planned), 80,000 are on the network and can communicate with each other across the world. "It's one of our biggest sales tools," boasts an executive. "Networking like this makes the world smaller, but tougher for manufacturers." **Kodak** also now uses electronic mail, and in the US—and soon in Europe—a computerized voice message system with an answer-back facility. This, European research director Bob Worden considers, "has changed our communications style in a revolutionary manner in the past five years. There are no more telephone messages. Even so, a lot of improvements are still needed in management information." One of the benefits of electronic mail over the telephone that he has noted (apart from time and labor savings) is that the system alleviates the language problem: because executives with a weak command of English can save the messages on their personal computers, they have the opportunity to clarify the meaning and compose an appropriate reply.

Evidently, the benefits of sophisticated IT systems are not going to be realized without very different styles of operation, just as the style of operation cannot be changed without major improvements to the IT system. "If you have a good network," considers IBM Europe's director of organization, Agnès Roux-Kiener, "you can have 25 people reporting in to one manager. We've managed to cut out two layers of management between the salesman and the chief executive." IBM is still working on its internal information system—"the rules and document system are being developed; everything has to be consistent."

However, Mike Perkin of Oasis warns:

> There's a growing realization that the technical developments are the easy bit. What is harder is to change the way people work. The shakeup affects everyone and is very painful. You will get gaps and things falling through them, so you have to be doubly clear why the new structure is good. I'm optimistic—I see a greater willingness after a reorganization to share information and work as a team. But what we've found is that companies need the same marketing skills internally as they use externally: What is the product, the system, the information process, job roles, threats and so on? Why should the staff buy it? How should the product be adapted to win the internal market?

In two recent restructuring cases he has been involved with, "the benefits have yet to show through. The companies haven't lost, but they haven't yet gained. They're convinced they're on the right course." This survey suggests that there is a growing realization among companies that unless they manage to extract the benefits offered by IT and the associated structural changes, they will face a serious and increasing competitive disadvantage.

Distribution and Administration

A corollary of the radical changes in the information flow round the sales and marketing structures is the implication for companies' order processing and warehousing operations. Both, of course, are integral parts of the information network, but once common systems have been established in Europe or even throughout the group, the processing points can be placed anywhere in the network, offering further opportunities for dispersion of the central management.

The internal market should see the dismantling of large numbers of regulations that have so far obstructed multinational distribution. As **NCR**'s Newall complains, "It's relatively easy to move goods from country to country; it's the secondary moves and adjustments that are the problem." NCR is therefore planning a centralized distribution system using just-in-time (JIT) techniques to keep inventory levels to a minimum. Similarly, with administration, "there's no reason why we shouldn't bill everyone from Amsterdam, say." American Express does that already, from its computer center in Brighton, on England's south coast. But it foresees the day when only the data base is central; the generation of accounts could be localized.

Rank Xerox, too, is planning a JIT distribution system based on its factory at Venray in southern Holland, with the aim of distributing its copiers direct from there to the customer. For the French small-appliances company **Moulinex,** the priorities and product sizes may be different but the need to rationalize the system is just as great. Group sales director Gilbert Torelli says that the newly revitalized company is considering all variables of the marketing mix—products, pricing, advertising, distribution—and "I'm sure that distribution is going to be the biggest factor. When I talk about logistics, at the moment we have warehouses everywhere, in each country. Depending on how things develop, perhaps we eventually won't need that."

Black & Decker is not alone in seeing distribution as a positive, competitive weapon, and in the opinion of European head Roger Thomas, there is no reason to accept current standards—"warehousing is an admission of failure." At the moment, says Thomas, "we can give stores a three-day service, but why not a 24-hour service—and can we do it from only three or four warehouses?"

Ironically, **ICI** reckons its distribution system gives it a competitive edge at the moment because it is rather better at negotiating the obstacles than its chemical competitors. When the barriers come down, that advantage will disappear, but this will give the company the opportunity to cut the number of warehouses, clerical staff and the time taken between receipt of order and delivery to the customer—of critical importance with effect chemicals, where (unlike commodities) daily orders and 24-hour delivery are accepted as normal.

The personal dimension

However a company's information system is organized, its efficient functioning depends on the people operating it. Some of the human issues concerning sales and marketing structures are examined in more detail in the next chapter.

Chapter 10

The Human Factor

Any corporate restructuring exacts a heavy price in personnel terms, and in Europewide restructuring, the price may be even heavier. New structures depend for their success on the ability of executives to embrace the new methods and to realize the benefits. Companies have to recognize that not everyone is suited to the kind of organization that they need to build up, either because of the nature of the organization itself, or an inability to take a broad international view. As a result, radical organizational change may imply a change of some of the personnel needed to run the operation.

Whatever the precise nature of the hurdles, most of the companies in this survey have gone to some lengths to help their staff jump over them. The fundamental changes announced by BP in early 1990 were the result of more than nine months of meetings among senior and middle managers to explain its intentions. The reorganization of Thorn EMI's lighting division came out of careful planning by the group's personnel and organization development director and three days of meetings among the managers to thrash out the details. It was ironic that the whole division was sold shortly afterward. If these two companies operated in only one country, the changes would be testing enough for corporate systems and the executives running them. The fact that the foreign dimension adds several more layers of complexity makes them traumatic.

Oasis consultant Mike Perkin, who specializes in the implementation of major information technology and reorganization projects, finds that "the shakeup can be very painful. The senior staff can usually cope because they can see and understand the final result. But the middle and junior staff can only see part of it and are in a much more difficult position. People cling to their geographical identity, and when that goes, their drive and commitment go. So the management has to be doubly clear why the new structure is good, and the messages have to be sold to the staff."

For companies not involved in quite such cataclysmic changes, the personnel issues are still important. "We have a heritage of too much diversity, and we have to stress the commonality now," says Colgate-Palmolive European president Brian Bergin. "We probably should bring people in, but that's difficult. So we prefer to remake ourselves, to look first among our own people. But we have to find a mechanism to achieve the same effect."

Some companies in this survey have already established a strong cooperative culture, often traceable back to the company's origins. Electrolux, Nestlé, Canon, NCR and Kodak all display a sense of corporate teamwork—a "roundtable in the mind," as the executive in another Japanese company described it (see Chapter 1). It is a quality that lends itself naturally to participation in international, flexible project teams and networks that global competition and IT appear to demand.

It is also a quality associated with ponderous bureaucracy at a time when the world markets are demanding speedy, flexible reactions, profit consciousness and lean management. The traditional power of well-motivated country managers is effective as long as markets can be considered in isolation; centralized structures work well for capital and research-intensive industries where the customer accepts what is offered. In searching for the best of all worlds, companies find that the solution lies as much in the executive's mind as in the structure and direction. Electrolux, Kodak and some others believe they have now got the balance about right. The record will provide the only final answer.

Meanwhile, for the many other companies that, like Colgate-Palmolive, believe they have some way to go before achieving that balance, staff issues in one form or another do loom large. At Hoechst, for example, its radical decentralization program—into autonomous business units, many of them outside Germany—has been delayed by a shortage of suitably experienced managers. ICI and Levi Straus have noted a significant increase in the reluctance of executives to move with the job. Perhaps the younger generation is, in some cases anyway, better prepared for a career in a European, rather than an American, German, French or any other business culture, but they have to be recruited with that view in mind, and that takes time.

Creating the Eurovision

It is partly for these reasons that many companies are spending more time on ways to increase the European vision and responsibilities of their executives, but with the minimum of disruption. The obvious step of simply transferring executives for a few years from their home subsidiaries to some others is relatively rare in the companies in this report—judging by actions rather than intentions. The growing number of wives with careers of their own, and the continuing problems of finding appropriate (and perhaps affordable) schooling for children are decisive factors for many executives.

Managements also face the sensitivities of local staff, the difficulties of career planning, and ensuring that executives can operate effectively on their foreign assignments and again when they return home. In some cases, there is simply a lack of the necessary central mechanism. The largest MNCs naturally find the process easier, and companies like ICI and Unilever have been transferring staff for years. However, even in these companies, staff transfers might need to be accelerated. "Transfers are an attempt to break down the feudalism—if the country manager's got a foreign marketing director, he can't count on his loyalty any more," said one consultant.

Developing Euromanagers

Roche, when it transfers staff, asserts that it simply aims to increase cooperation inside the group. A senior executive says the company "wants its managers to have experience in different areas, not just in sales and marketing. Roche wants to create Euromanagers who have developed international experience through six-month to two-year assignments. International experience counts for a lot in determining management potential."

L'Oréal is also a staff transfer enthusiast. Assistant director for consumer products Giles Roger claims: "Twenty years ago, a marketing director in France would hear from local marketing directors that 'things are different here.' But now everything is international, modern . . . because of European culture and the fact that we move around. European culture is being disseminated in the universities, the schools . . . when people come to us now, they already have three languages."

There may be an element of Gallic enthusiasm in that response. Some companies find French and Italian executives the most reluctant of all Europeans to live outside their home countries. Further, a career with a foreign multinational, with a promotion ladder leading inexorably toward Frankfurt or New York, may hold less attraction than some national institution, particularly for graduates of the elite French *grandes ecoles*. Other nationalities, however cosmopolitan, face similar dilemmas, and **Honeywell,** while it expects its staff to be ready to live anywhere in Europe and would not normally appoint someone to a general management position without foreign experience, finds it necessary nonetheless to guarantee to move them back home afterward.

A readiness to work in other countries for longer or shorter periods has always been a condition of employment for some companies with extensive overseas interests. The difference in Europe is that working in Milan or Malmö is coming to be regarded as equivalent to home. "The highly successful executives accept that their home countries can't satisfy them," claims Jean-Pierre Rosso, Honeywell's European president, himself French but having spent most of his career in either the US or Belgium.

Introducing European and local responsibilities

The problems may be more acute for the middle fliers. Companies' top priority must always be to find and develop good business managers, but a facility for languages, and just as important, a sympathy with and understanding of other countries' cultures and customs are naturally of growing importance. In practice, most companies find that much can be achieved with a gradualist policy, which may actually help solve other personnel problems, as Union Carbide explains:

Local salesmen often need to be offered further career opportunities but may not wish to transfer to another country, so some of the more senior people are given a European assignment as well. It is very motivating and not too expensive. In Germany, one salesman spends 30% of his time on the one product line for which he has European responsibility—this allows him to travel, breaks him in gently to international work—but he still keeps his major responsibility at home and does not have to be transferred to Geneva. This way he can see if he is really ready for international work.

Giving an executive a European as well as a national hat in this way is gaining in popularity for several reasons:

- It adds to the individual's job opportunities.

- It exposes him to the international dimension.

- It promotes the transfer of valuable ideas and skills between subsidiaries.

- It helps avoid the "not invented here" mentality.

- It saves the rising costs of transferring executives to another country, and the overheads of another layer of management.

Inevitably, however, companies have also encountered a number of drawbacks:

- Responsibilities may become confused and rapid remedial action more difficult.

- The executive's prime role in his home subsidiary may be neglected.

- Salary and other costs may need to be apportioned, the system for which may be unavoidably complicated.

- The company management information system may need an overhaul to give the executive the data needed for him to take on the additional work.

- Considerable time may be spent in traveling and liaison meetings.

- New developments will take longer to spread round the group if one or two executives are relied on to take them from one subsidiary to the next.

For most companies, the pros are considered to outweigh the cons, and **American Express,** for one, makes extensive use of the system of giving staff additional, external responsibilities (see Chapter 5). The UK subsidiary may earn fees for the time its executives spend helping its European fellows, and according to the UK managing director, Alan Stark, "the fees do well for both sides," since the paying company saves the salaries of local experts. For the future, Amex is recruiting "international-type MBAs to become a Europewide management resource," but Stark finds that "although some sell themselves as European managers, they are not necessarily any better." At a more senior level, Amex has a "very valuable" group of managers who move from market to market, although the corporate policy is to employ national staff wherever possible—"I'm the first Brit in this job," remarks Stark.

3M as usual has pushed the system one step further. As well as giving suitable executives European assignments either individually or as a member of a team in "resource sharing programs," executives with potential are given the accolade of "subsidiary-based international managers." The formal identification acts as some incentive in itself, and they meet every year in Brussels to learn more about and discuss 3M's European progress and strategy. "We've still got a long way to go," thinks European vice president Edoardo Pieruzzi, "but I think we're on the move."

Other companies seem to share his optimism. **Reckitt & Colman,** through its quarterly marketing meetings and a lead country system, finds that "people's attitudes have changed. They're concentrating on the similarities, not the differences. You have to persist at harmonization, and moving from complexity to simplicity." **Heinz** now claims that its "thinking is much less insular—it's the sort of nonparochial thinking on every subject that we're trying to instill." Information technology networks will help the process on: "I want operating managers to see what's happening in Italy and France," says Heinz's European senior vice president Paul Corddry. Equally, personal attitudes, skills and interest will be necessary to make the IT systems provide the benefits that they promise. Managing through project teams and through the network will make big demands on individuals' flexibility and adaptability.

Rewarding the Good Europeans

Most companies accept that the system of rewards for its senior staff has a powerful part to play in shaping attitudes to a European structure. Country managers with large bonuses dependent on the profits of their subsidiaries cannot be expected to have much enthusiasm for changes that may strengthen the company but make bonuses harder to earn. Equally, a single group bonus is unlikely to be much of a motivator since the manager can do little to influence the outcome. Most companies in the survey (one exception is Moulinex where, following the management buyout, a large number of the employees hold shares) regard motivation of key individuals as vital, and one of the arguments for keeping national subsidiaries intact is that they provide a performance focus around which some kind of bonus system can be maintained. The trick is to ensure that local rewards do not undermine Europewide profits—neatly summing up the whole European structure debate.

Highly decentralized companies can afford to make country managers' bonuses dependent entirely on the results of their operations. Few, however, would go as far as the UK electronic instrumentation group **Eurotherm**, which has a policy of setting up an individual manager with a sizable stake in a new subsidiary in a new market, and even establishing arm's-length transfer prices to ensure that the profits are realistic and the motivation fair and effective. The system works well, but the managers concerned are not expected to cooperate with each other in the way that most of the larger companies in this report regard as essential.

Instead, some more complex reward system has to be found that will reflect and encourage the fulfillment of the central strategy. **Roche** managers are rewarded for performance against a number of factors, including budget achievement, launching of new products, staff development and profitability. But while each of those factors is calculated only on the performance of the subsidiary or business unit, the system cannot be said to encourage cooperation. Some companies have therefore settled for a combination of national and European or group bonuses.

Heinz goes one stage further, linking a substantial part of its European chief executives' rewards to a formula based on volume, profit and return on investment (ROI). Down the line, a formula is used linking total profits and individual goals according to a 15-point scale:

- 2 points corporate profit;
- 2 points European subsidiary group performance;
- 5 points individual subsidiary performance; and
- 6 points individual performance.

The European subsidiary performance has only recently been inserted to encourage the European as well as the group and national company performance. The product line heads also receive bonuses based on profit and ROI, and the company has probably made more use of stock options among its staff than any other comparable US company. Some 16% of the equity is now in employee hands, and "every key player in the organization is an owner of the company," says Corddry. "It ensures they focus on the corporate good, not their own affiliate. In meetings, when they discuss, say, the reallocation of marketing funds, people say 'OK, let's do it. It'll affect my stock price.'"

The Pleasures of Travel?

Closer coordination of European operations, however achieved, unavoidably demands more traveling by key staff, and several companies in the report make it clear that for many executives, this is a growing charge on their time. A certain amount of traveling may be desirable from a corporate as well as a personal point of view. "Managing by walking around" has a long and honorable tradition, and many executives point out that the alternative to going to see for oneself is far worse. The sharp differences in conditions and attitudes across Europe demand regular visits by managers if they are to do their job properly. For every executive who travels too much, there will be one who travels too little.

John Ankeny, Levi Strauss's marketing services director, spends 85% of his time away from his Brussels base, visiting the European subsidiaries or the US headquarters. NCR's European senior vice president Fred Newall spends less than half his time in Europe, the rest fulfilling his role as a corporate NCR officer in Dayton Ohio. The US and Japanese MNCs are at an obvious disadvantage in this respect, particularly where the European head has to present his region's case at headquarters as well as traveling round the European subsidiaries.

The same problem afflicts the Europeans, however. At Electrolux and Reckitt & Colman, some senior executives spend a third or half of their time visiting their European outposts, and Moulinex, with its new ambition to strengthen its European position and image, is heading in the same direction. With the growth of international team working, dual responsibilities and management networks, the need for middle ranks of executives to travel more frequently is also growing, encouraged by companies anxious to break down the national barriers.

Too much travel easily becomes a burden for the executive and his family. It can sap his energy as well as absorb large amounts of time, leaving him incommunicado for long periods and beyond management control. A heavy travel schedule, with its macho, hands-on image, can easily be mistaken for the reality of management, and can merely leave the local executives bemused and alienated. It has been dubbed by one critic as "pigeon management," where the executive flies in, leaves a mess and flies out.

It may be that developments in information technology will save some traveling, either by providing more data and message systems direct to executives' terminals or through tele-conferencing facilities. But for the time being at least, the need for executives at all levels to travel throughout Europe and beyond is likely to grow, with Central and Eastern Europe adding more markets, with their own peculiarities to be mastered. Meanwhile, the increasing congestion on the European air routes, as well as at the approaches to major cities, can be expected to exacerbate the problems. In fact, the effective span of European management may in future be limited more by airline schedules than by an executive's capacity to control and lead subordinates.

Adopting a realistic approach

Companies' only remedy may be to take a more realistic view of the need to travel, or even to modify their structures and procedures. Either way, the fact that they are, in the end, made up of groups of people who need to be led, encouraged and made to feel wanted will ensure that there is an irreducible minimum of travel to be undertaken.

There can be no question that the effectiveness of companies' sales and marketing structures depends first and last on the people in them, and travel has a direct contribution to make. But it should not be allowed to obscure the deeper personnel issues which all of the developments outlined in this report are exposing. Recognizing and tackling them is a prerequisite for success in Europe.

Part IV

Conclusions

Chapter 11

Conclusions

Restructuring has now become an ever-present feature of corporate life. The fact that well over half of the companies in this survey have significantly altered their European marketing and sales structures in the past two years is sufficient indication of how seriously the matter is being taken as global competitive pressures mount and the shape of commercial Europe changes with every passing month. The reconstruction of the Central and East European economies (given reasonable political stability) and the lowering of barriers in Western Europe are likely to act as continuous stimuli to structural change for companies resolved to keep their place in world markets.

Concentration or fragmentation?

These developments seem likely to give an added impetus to the trend for the bigger companies to grow, relative to smaller and medium-sized concerns. It is significant that the giant Philips has taken a 25% stake in the specialist Bang & Olufsen to tap into its European marketing expertise; and that Thorn EMI, in spite of earlier corporate conclusions that lighting would form one of its strategic core businesses, which it therefore strengthened with £200 million worth of acquisitions, decided it could not compete effectively in world lighting markets and nearly sold the whole bundle to the US electrical giant GTE.

Even so, it is salutary to remember that confident predictions that world markets would soon be dominated by a few very large companies have been made for decades, but have yet to be fulfilled. Even IBM's hold on the computer market no longer seems as unshakable as it once was, mainly for the reason that as markets and technologies change, so do the factors that favored the original dominance of one or two companies.

As markets develop, there is a natural tendency for them to fragment, as consumers become more discriminating and marketers more successful in developing variants to tempt them. The giants can keep on top in these circumstances only at the expense of increasing organizational complexity, and the elaborate moves outlined in this report to rationalize the range of products with the number of national markets is an indication of the problems their managements face. It may be that in some markets, the complexities will prove to form an upper limit on growth: Electrolux for one could well be reaching that point.

Aiming for decentralization

Contrary to some predictions, centralizing corporate power is not a favored solution. Only a quarter of the surveyed companies that had changed their organizations mentioned increased centralization as one of the objectives, with the rest opting either for decentralization or some

Organizing for Marketing Advantage
Business International

kind of matrix. These terms are, of course, relative in some degree—any change in a highly centralized company could probably be described as increasing autonomy—and they reflect intention rather than action. But the hard experience of companies, as revealed here, is at odds with the absolutist prescriptions of some consultants.

While the arguments about the similarities and differences between European markets are likely to continue for many years yet, there is little doubt in most respondents' minds that companies and their structures have to cater for both, extracting the maximum benefit from the similarities as well as taking maximum advantage of the differences. But perhaps more significant for the organizational issue are all of the other characteristics of individual markets that determine market share—distribution, sales customs, usage rates, advertising practice, discounts etc.—and demand close local attention.

Moving toward networks

None of the companies in the survey yet makes significant use of management networks—not to be confused with information technology (IT) networks on the one hand, or the grapevine on the other. There is, however, a distinct move toward more informal organizational links, which cut across traditional departmental boundaries in order to tackle particular problems and developments. It is not too fanciful to see this method of working evolving into some sort of "intelligent" network where executives across Europe work closely together on marketing and sales programs without having to report their every move and seek approval up through the hierarchy. Such a development depends vitally on two factors:

☐ The rapid reorganization in management information systems and heavy investment in the IT delivery networks are needed to give executives access to reliable and comprehensive corporate data, and allow them to communicate with each other. Few of the companies in this report are adequately equipped in that respect, and the resources required in cash and management time to bring their systems up to the standard required are daunting.

☐ The training and experience of the executives concerned are also critical. Companies have found that, however expensive, rewiring is the easy bit: much more difficult is training and motivating executives to adopt the new ways of working. A large component of that is the nature and degree of supervision required to ensure that the system produces the desired result.

Promoting corporate compromise

For some time to come, therefore, companies are likely to persevere with variants around the organizational themes described here—a small central authority, profit-accountable country managers whose operations are drawn together by a number of detailed links ranging from perhaps a formal matrix with European product managers and account managers, through European brand groups to ad hoc committees, task forces and individual executives with dual roles. The physical location of the key players will decrease in importance as companies struggle to find and keep the best available talent. The executives will achieve closer coordination across Europe on issues like product specification, pricing and advertising, but have more say in formulating the decisions and strategies that they implement.

ACTION CHECKLIST: HOW DOES YOUR ORGANIZATION MEASURE UP?

Looked at from the center, does your European organization:

➤ Reflect and support the company's manufacturing and marketing strategy for the EC, Efta, and Central and Eastern Europe, and offer the means of applying it?

➤ Provide a clear view of actual and potential sales, market share, and profit by product and by country?

➤ Allow a rapid change of direction or emphasis should the market or other circumstances demand it?

➤ Allow ideas and resources to be focused on the product/territory offering the best prospects?

➤ Allow central managers to spot the talent and the best practice, and utilize them throughout the group?

➤ Draw key executives across Europe into decisions affecting European business as a whole?

➤ Motivate them to take a European and corporate view by appropriate reward systems?

➤ Involve the minimum number of layers of management?

➤ Support more flexible ways of cooperative working such as task forces, either directly or through the corporate culture?

➤ Provide uniform financial data and allow the benefits of information technology to be realized?

➤ Facilitate growth by acquisition and joint venture?

Looked at from the field, does your organization:

➤ Provide the cost benefits of central sourcing without the penalties of delays, inflexibility etc.?

➤ Provide marketing support from elsewhere in the group when needed?

➤ Allow an effective local input to central product planning so that the product range is appropriate to local conditions?

➤ Allow fast and effective response to local market conditions?

➤ Recognize local excellence through lead country status, dual national/European roles etc.?

➤ Ensure that good product and marketing ideas are deployed rapidly?

➤ Provide a base for multinational marketing activities such as market research, advertising, sponsorship etc.?

➤

Organizing for Marketing Advantage
Business International

> ➤ Mobilize corporate expertise to serve multinational customers effectively in each country?

> ➤ Allow rational and effective bidding for public-sector contracts?

> ➤ Allow the right balance to be struck in pricing between European coordination and local flexibility?

> ➤ Supply accurate and timely data on market trends and performance?

The picture is one of compromise, therefore, between the earlier extremes of centralized marketing and sales control on the one hand, and decentralized autonomy on the other. In most markets, neither is appropriate any longer. Many companies can join IBM in claiming to have effected a real shift in the center of corporate power down the hierarchy and nearer to the individual market. The changing nature of some markets as well as tougher competition demands much closer cooperation with the customer, which can be achieved only at the local level. But the loose, autonomous confederations of marketing and sales companies that have long catered for Europe's multifarious needs are no longer adequate to meet global competition and fast-changing consumer preferences.

Keeping options open

The big losers in all of these changes are the middle ranks of managers and executives, who have lost influence and often their jobs to the field operations in one direction, and to the center in the other. The field operations demand greater flexibility and support to outwit competitors in the battle for the customer's favor. The center has to have recourse to acquisitions, joint ventures and various forms of cooperation in the search for ways to expand into new technologies and markets. More power therefore has to be concentrated at the center, ready for quick decisions when the opportunity occurs. If companies are to extract profitable growth from the vast but enigmatic European market in the 1990s, they need to pursue all avenues with energy and conviction.